Study!

A guide to effective learning, revision and examination techniques

Second Edition

Robert Barrass

ROUTLEDGE
Taylor & Francis Group

London and New York

First published 1984 by Chapman & Hall Ltd
Reprinted 1985, 1991, 1994, 1996

Reprinted 2001
by Routledge
11 New Fetter Lane, London EC4P 4EE

Simultaneously published in the USA and Canada
by Routledge
29 West 35th Street, New York, NY 10001

Reprinted 2000, 2001

Second edition first published 2002

Routledge is an imprint of the Taylor & Francis Group

© 1984, 2002 Robert Barrass

Typeset by RefineCatch Limited, Bungay, Suffolk
Printed and bound in Great Britain by
TJ International Ltd, Padstow, Cornwall

British Library Cataloguing in Publication Data
A catalogue record for this book is available from the British Library

Library of Congress Cataloging in Publication Data
A catalog record for this book is available from the British Library

ISBN 0–415–26995–4

Contents

Preface   xi
Definition of terms   xii
Acknowledgements   xiii

Part 1 Accepting responsibility for your learning

1 Study: rules for the game   3
Why study?   3
Are all your subjects interesting?   5
Do you study effectively?   6
  Study skills   7

2 Look after yourself   10
Looking after yourself   10
  Deciding where to live   10
  Looking after your money   11
  Avoiding anxiety about your work   12
  Asking for help with study problems   14
Keeping fit for study   14
  Exercise and health   15
  Food and health   16
  Sleep and health   16
  Friendship   16
  Being yourself   17
  Personal relationships   20
  Coping with personal problems   21

3 Make good use of your time | 23
Accept responsibility for your learning | 23
Organise your year | 26
Organise your week | 28
Organise your day | 33
Concentrate during hours of study | 36

Part 2 Student centred learning

4 Listen and learn | 45
Being there | 45
The value of lectures in study | 46
Make notes as you listen | 49
Sequential notes | 51
Creative pattern notes | 54
Other kinds of notes | 55
Get into the habit of asking good questions | 56
After the lecture | 57
Review | 58
Revise | 59
Get the most out of group work | 59
Tutorials | 59
Seminars | 60
Self-help groups | 62
Writing paper and storage materials | 63
Writing paper | 64
Storing your notes | 64

5 Think and learn | 66
Organise and select | 66
How to remember | 67
Revise regularly | 68
Learn some things by heart | 69
Use your knowledge | 70
Plan answers to questions | 71
Exercise your mind | 75

6 Observe and learn | 77
Difficulties in the way of accurate observation | 77

Contents

Make notes as you observe 82
Results of the analysis of data 83
Preparing a report on an investigation 84

7 **Read and learn** 85
Decide what to read 86
  Preliminary survey 86
Decide how to read 87
  Scanning 88
  Skim reading 88
  Rapid reading 89
  Reading critically 89
Make notes as you read 91
  One set of notes 95
Understand and select 96
  Comprehension tests 96
  Writing a précis 96
  Writing a summary 97
Get to know useful sources of information 98
  Reference books and journals 98
  The Internet (World Wide Web) 102
  Intranets 104
Open learning 105
  Resources for courses 105
  Computer-based learning 105
  Computer assisted learning 105

8 **Write and learn** 109
Faults commonly encountered in students' written work 110
Write answers to questions 117
  Creativity 117
  Write at one sitting 119
  Use your topic outline as a guide 120
Criticise the work of other writers 121
  See how others write 122
Check your own work 124
How course work marks affect your grades 124
Writing and learning 127

9 Express yourself   131
    Writing about your subject   131
        Write in paragraphs   132
        Write in sentences   132
        Take an interest in words   134
        Write regularly and read good prose   141
        Write legibly   141
    Talking about your subject   142
        Preparing a short talk (or presentation)   142
        Visual aids   144
        Giving your talk   146

10 Working on a special study   147
    Deciding what to study   147
    How your work will be assessed   149
    Working on your own   149
    Reporting your work   151
        Planning your composition   153
        Starting to write   155
        Reviewing the literature   156
        Preparing diagrams and tables   157
        Writing for your readers   157
        Preparing the typescript   158

Part 3 Revision and examination techniques

11 Preparing for tests and examinations   163
    Consider what is expected of you   163
    Use appropriate textbooks   165
    Look at syllabuses and course guides   165
    Look at recent examination papers   166
    Plan answers to examination questions   166
    Prepare revision aids from your notes   167
    Test yourself   169
    Plan your revision   170
        The weeks before an examination   171

12 Taking tests and examinations   **174**
  Taking tests as part of course work   174
    Answering questions in tests   175
  Taking examinations   176
    Learn from other students' mistakes   177
    Learn from your own mistakes   186
    Well prepared and ready to start   187
    Taking a theory examination   188
    Taking a practical examination   191
    Taking an oral examination   192
    Failing an examination   193

Appendix A Choosing a course   **195**
  Distance learning   196
  Disadvantages of distance learning   196
  Advantages of distance learning   197
  Studying part-time   198
  Studying full-time   198

Appendix B Computer appreciation   **200**
  Using your computer   200
  Word processing   200
  Looking after your documents   203
  Looking after yourself when using a computer   204
  Making more use of your computer   205
  Desk top publishing   206
  Preparing presentations   206
  Using spreadsheets   206
  Preparing and using a database   207
  Purchasing a computer   208

Appendix C Further reading   **209**
  Books for your bookshelf   209
  References (publications cited in the text)   211

Index   **212**

Preface

Students of all subjects are judged by their performance in course work, tests and examinations, yet most are given little or no advice on study, revision or examination techniques. Most tutors give advice only when they see that it is needed, and many students devote much time to learning but give little thought to improving their study skills. They continue to use the methods of learning that contributed to their success – or limited their success – at school. They learn from their own mistakes – if these are recognised – and pick up advice about study, here and there, as they go along.

Left to themselves many students learn to study effectively, but they may take several months to adjust to the differences between school and college or university. They continue to gather ideas and to improve their study skills throughout their student life, and so are much better students by the end of their course than they were at the beginning. However, many still have much to learn about study, revision and examination techniques at the end of their course. It is as if they had come to the end of the game and were still learning the rules. They may then feel, even if they worked hard, that they have not achieved their full potential.

Students who know that they are not doing as well as they could in assessed course work, tests and examinations, although they are working hard, are likely to benefit most from straightforward advice – because they know they need help. But students who are satisfied with their progress can also be helped to do even better work, just as talented athletes can improve their performance when well coached. So it would be best if all students, in the first few weeks of their course, were to consider how to use their study and leisure time. Learning to work effectively (improving their ability to think, understand, select, organise, explain and remember) would help them not only as students but also in any career.

The advice in this guide to effective learning is to help students to think about the way they learn and, where necessary to improve their study, revision and examination techniques. They may read it chapter by chapter (rather than at one sitting) during the first weeks of a course, and then try the techniques recommended. Afterwards they may refer to appropriate chapters, for advice on particular points, throughout their course.

There have been many changes in higher education in the twenty years since I began work on the first edition of this guide. First, more students are now returning to study after a period of paid employment; more are working part-time to finance their full-time studies; and more are continuing their studies part-time while in full-time employment. Second, most students now use computers to help them with their learning – for information retrieval, for data analysis, and for word processing. And third, there is more emphasis on student centred learning, partly as a result of the increased use of computers. In this revised edition I have taken account of these developments, but have not made changes just for the sake of change. Tutors familiar with the first edition, who recommend this guide to their students, use it as an aid to counselling, or use it as a text to support their courses on effective learning or study skills, should therefore still find the information and advice that contributed to the success of the first edition and that continues to be relevant to students' needs. As in the first edition, suggestions for class work are listed in the index after the entry *Exercises and discussion topics*.

DEFINITION OF TERMS

Because the following terms have different meanings in different countries, and even in different institutions in one country, they are defined here.

Assessor or *marker*: one who assesses the merit of a work and assigns a grade or mark.
Teachers: all those who teach in a school, college or university.
Lecturers and *tutors*: people who give lectures and tutorials in a

college (although many of them have other titles such as doctor and professor).

School or *high school*: an institution where pupils, up to the age of eighteen, take introductory courses.

College: an institution (college or university) where students take advanced courses.

Term: a period at college, between vacations (one third of an academic year).

Semester: half an academic year.

Class: any short organised period of instruction.

Module or *course unit*: a distinct part of a course of study, assessed separately from other units or modules included in the same course.

ACKNOWLEDGEMENTS

I thank Jonathan Barrass for help in preparing this second edition, especially with the parts on aspects of information technology. I also thank Elizabeth Cunningham, independent IT Trainer and Consultant for reading the typescript for Appendix 3, and colleagues in the University of Sunderland: Library staff for help with information retrieval, Paul Griffin and Richard Hall of the School of Sciences for their interest and for advice on the use of personal computers and on health and safety, respectively, and Beverley Morgan of Learning Development Services for reading and commenting on the whole book in typescript. I also thank Ann, my wife, for her help and encouragement, and Adrian Burrows who drew the cartoons.

Some examples of unclear writing are quoted, with concise comments. As in the first edition, and like Gowers (see page 210), I do not acknowledge the sources of such extracts – but none is from the work of a student and some are from publications by senior academics.

University of Sunderland   Robert Barrass
14 July 2001

Part 1

Accepting responsibility for your learning

Different people study effectively in different ways, so no one can tell you how to study, but knowing about ways of working that others have found useful should help you to improve your own study skills. You haven't time to learn only by experience, by making and correcting mistakes.

Obviously, the best time to review your study, revision and examination techniques is at the beginning of your course. You are likely to find the techniques used at school, where you were taught, are not good enough at college or university – where it is up to you to take responsibility for your learning – and you will want to do as well as you can from the start of your course.

1

Study: rules for the game

WHY STUDY?

Whatever your reason for continuing or resuming your studies, make the most of this opportunity to participate in college life, to develop your personality, to undertake more demanding studies of subjects in which you are already interested, to develop your ability to think, and to take examinations which will provide a challenge and a measure of your achievement.

Many students who withdraw from a course early, or fail in their examinations, do so because they are not well motivated. Think carefully, therefore, before deciding upon the kind of course to take (see Appendix A) and before deciding which subjects to study in each year of your course. Then remember that you are taking this course and studying these subjects because you chose to do so.

To maintain your sense of purpose it is best to have clear long- and short-term goals (see Figure 1.1). For example:

Long term: to progress in a particular career; to achieve grades at the end of your course that are a true reflection of your ability.

Short term: to devote enough time to recreation including your social life; to attend all classes; to complete homework on time; to do your best work.

Immediate: to recognize things that need your attention; to arrange these tasks in order of priority; and then to concentrate on one task at a time.

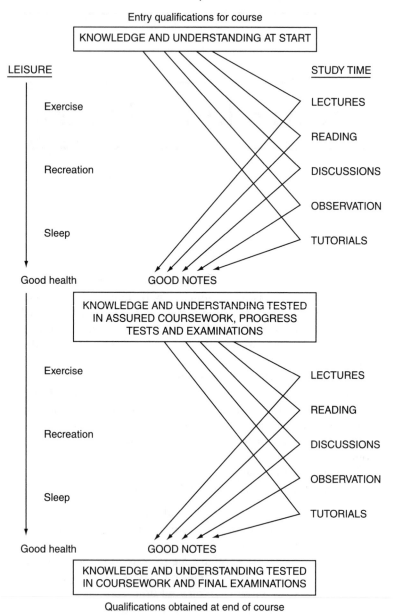

Figure 1.1 Charting your path through a college course.

ARE ALL YOUR SUBJECTS INTERESTING?

You will probably find some subjects interesting from the start, but others may not immediately seem relevant to your main subjects. Consider why these are part of your course. Recognise their importance to you; appreciate their relevance to everyday life or to different careers. Try to relate them to things in which you are already interested, and remember that they probably do provide a foundation for more advanced work in which you intend to specialise later in your course or as a career.

Most people encounter some difficulties when they start a new subject. For example, it may be necessary to learn new words and their meaning. You can develop a positive approach to your studies, in any subject, by being determined to master its special language and other fundamentals. One way or another, making an effort to learn about and understand a subject is your first step towards success in the subject.

You can develop your interest by devoting more time to a subject rather than less. If the lecturer does not capture your interest, look at relevant parts of your textbook which may provide a different approach. If you find your textbook hard-going, look at other books: you should be able to find one that is easier to understand and yet suited to your needs. If you still cannot understand, ask your tutor for help (see page 14).

Studying a subject is rather like fitting pieces into a jig-saw puzzle. It is easier to concentrate if you are interested, and as your interest grows you become more and more engrossed. The more you learn, the more you see the subject as a whole and the greater your understanding (see Figure 1.2). Mastering something that you at first found difficult also boosts your self-confidence in your ability to learn.

Pleasure in study comes from acquiring knowledge, from widening your experience, from developing your ability to solve problems or make judgements, and from your deeper understanding of, for example, works of literature or art, or of people, or of the world. Pleasure also comes from the better results achieved in course work and examinations.

Study!

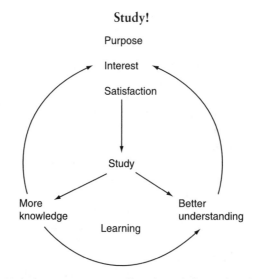

Figure 1.2 Links between interest, effort, knowledge and understanding.

DO YOU STUDY EFFECTIVELY?

Adopting effective study, revision and examination techniques is largely a matter of common sense: if someone suggests possible courses of action it is usually easy to decide which is likely to be the most effective. For example:

1 Do you sit trying to study but feel, after several hours (see Figure 1.3) that you have not achieved very much? Do you devote most time to the subjects in which most course work is set? Do you spend most time on your favourite subjects? Or do you work to a time-table, studying all subjects but spending most time (as suggested in this chapter) on those that most need your attention?
2 Do you think that being a good student is simply a matter of knowing how to study and how to communicate your knowledge and understanding? Or do you agree that it is just as important to look after yourself (see Chapter 2), and have a good social life (see Chapter 3), if you are to do your best work?

Study may be compared with a game: your purpose is not only to master your subjects but also to score points in course work and examinations. As in playing any game, the first step is to know the rules (see Figure 1.4).

WHAT SHALL I DO NEXT ?

Figure 1.3 Let your friends know when you will be studying – so that you will not be disturbed at these times.

Study skills

Part-time students must be well motivated, self-reliant, and able to work alone, but even full-time students should accept that they must take responsibility for their own learning. Whether you are studying part-time or full-time, think of yourself as working for a qualification rather than as being taught.

In addition to attending formal lectures and other organised classes, and sitting formal examinations, you will be assessed on the quality of your written course work: including short compositions and longer dissertations, extended essays, term papers, and project reports. The academic staff may advise, direct or supervise the work upon which these compositions are based, but these activities are intended to give students opportunities to develop their abilities: to

8   **Study!**

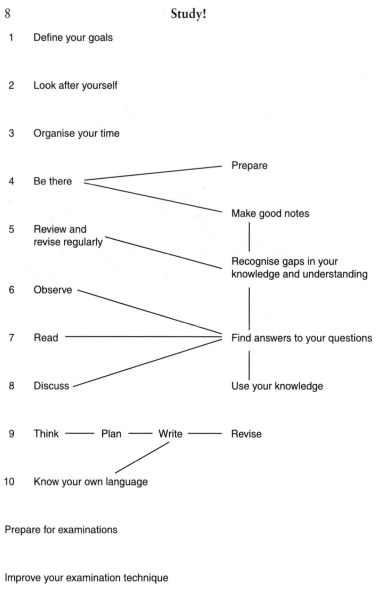

1   Define your goals

2   Look after yourself

3   Organise your time

4   Be there   Prepare

                                    Make good notes

5   Review and
     revise regularly

                                    Recognise gaps in your
                                    knowledge and understanding

6   Observe

7   Read   Find answers to your questions

8   Discuss   Use your knowledge

9   Think —— Plan —— Write —— Revise

10   Know your own language

Prepare for examinations

Improve your examination technique

Figure 1.4 Rules for study

organise their time, to think for themselves, to co-operate with others, to make use of libraries and other resources, and to communicate their thoughts in speech and in writing.

If your long-term objective in study is to achieve your full potential, you must develop not only your knowledge and understanding of the subjects you are studying, and your interest in these subjects, but also the *personal skills* which – because they are the basis for success in any subject – are called *core skills* or *study skills*. Because they are needed for success in all careers, they are also called *common skills*, *enterprise skills*, *key skills* or *transferable skills* (see Table 1.1). It is perhaps because their importance is recognised by people with different interests (academics, employers and customers – as well as students) that they are given so many different names.

Table 1.1 Some skills needed in studying any subject and in any career

Personal skills	Why some students under-achieve
1. Self management	Not working hard enough, or poorly directed effort. Overwork. Personal problems. Problems with relationships.
2. Money management	Budgeting problems. Worries about money.
3. Time management	Lack of planning: ineffective use of time for study, recreation and rest.
4. Summarising	Inability to distinguish important points from the supporting detail. Not making good notes in organised classes and in private study.
5. Finding information	Not making good use of libraries and other sources of ideas and information.
6. Processing information	Not bringing together relevant information and ideas from lectures, tutorials, seminars, practical work, background reading, and other sources.
7. Problem solving	Not thinking things through to a satisfactory conclusion.
8. Thinking and creativity	Mindless repetition of other people's thoughts: unwillingness to consider new approaches or different points of view.
9. Communicating	Not expressing thoughts clearly, concisely and convincingly when speaking and writing.

2

Look after yourself

At college or university you make a fresh start, with different people in unfamiliar surroundings. The methods of instruction are different from those used at school and you will need to adopt new techniques that help you to think, to learn and to communicate your thoughts. If you go straight from school to college you will probably look forward to making the break from being cared for to caring for your self, and enjoy the new experiences that provide both challenges and opportunities. If you are returning to full-time study after a period of other employment, or studying part-time while engaged in other employment, you will have to get used to being a student again – or to leading a double life – fitting study in with other your responsibilities. However, irrespective of your previous experience or your current responsibilities, to keep fit for study you must look after yourself.

LOOKING AFTER YOURSELF

Deciding where to live

Most colleges provide a good working environment. To study most effectively, good living accommodation is also necessary. Preferably you should have your own room in which you can relax by yourself, when you wish to do so, or study without distractions.

If you are away from home it is probably best to live with other students, in college accommodation, at least for your first year at college. This increases your opportunities to make friends with students who are studying different subjects – and so to broaden your interests. In this first year you will also get to know about other kinds of accommodation that may be available, and can consider their advantages and disadvantages. Wherever you live, you will need a place in which to study effectively – without spending too much time or money on travel. You will probably also want to take advantage of the opportunities for recreation and friendship that college life provides.

If you are studying part-time, or studying full-time at a local college, you will probably live at home and have no accommodation problems. However, changes in your living arrangement may be needed. For example, it is not possible to work effectively in a room shared with other people who are doing different things (such as talking, listening to the radio, watching television, or playing games). You will also need the encouragement and support of other members of your family. The same applies if you share accommodation with other students: you need appropriate conditions during the hours that must be devoted to private study.

If you cannot go into another room to study, when you are at home, try to fit as much of your study time as possible into your timetable so that you can work regularly in the reading room of a local library or in your college library. Then study at home at times when you expect other people to be out or busy in other rooms.

Looking after your money

If you have saved while in employment, so that you could attend college full-time, or have to work part-time so that you can afford to pursue your studies, you will have experience of budgeting and are unlikely to need advice. But if you have never been in paid employment, you may have responsibility for more money than has been available to you before.

If you have received a grant or award it is best to put your money into an account in which it will earn as much interest as possible, but from which withdrawals can be made either immediately or at short notice. Similarly, if you have access to a loan, it is best to withdraw no more than you really need: even an interest free loan has to be repaid. Estimate how much you must spend during the

term (for example, for accommodation, fuel, clothing, food, trans-
port, tuition and examination fees, books and stationery). Each
term deduct your estimated expenditure from the amount you could
afford to spend in the term, so that you have an idea of how much
you have available to spend on other things. You can then withdraw
a fixed amount each week – if you need it.

Avoiding anxiety about your work

Anxiety may arise in study because you have difficulty in concentrating, or sit trying to learn your notes but feel after much effort
that you cannot remember them, or have difficulty in completing
assignments to your own satisfaction in the time available, or feel
that you are just not coping with all the different things that must be
done. Such anxieties, which result from an ineffective use of time,
can usually be overcome, avoided, or relieved, by adopting an active
approach to study. Keeping up-to-date depends partly on application (devoting enough time to study and concentrating during
hours of study) and partly on organisation. So if you find yourself in
difficulties, consider what you may be doing wrong.

1 Do you need to change your attitude to study (see page 315)?
2 Do you need to improve your study skills?
3 Are you devoting too much or too little time to recreation?

It is natural, especially at the start of a new course, to wonder if
you will be able to cope with the more advanced work. However,
if you have the entry requirements for an advanced course, and if
you work hard, study effectively, and have enough recreation, you
should succeed in the course and achieve a grade that is a true
reflection of your ability. If at first you score low marks in course
work, or do not do as well as you expected, do not be discouraged.
You have to get used to new methods of working and higher standards. Be positive: try to see where you went wrong so that you can
do better next time.

For any student, anxiety about work that has still to be done may
result in too much time being devoted to study – in an attempt to
catch up. But overworking, by definition, is counterproductive.
Overwork can result in less being achieved, in each hour of study,
than would otherwise be possible. Also, overwork can itself be a
symptom and then a cause of anxiety. Study will sometimes

encroach on your leisure time but do not allow study to become a habit to the extent that you do not take necessary breaks. And do not worry in your leisure time because there are tasks awaiting your attention: this too is counterproductive. In study there are always things to be done, and you can avoid anxiety by concentrating on one task at a time and completing the most urgent tasks first.

Do not worry if you feel that you read too slowly and will never be able to read all the things that you are expected to read. Be assured that any student who has passed the qualifying examinations (fulfilling the entrance requirements for an advanced course) is unlikely to be handicapped by slow reading (see page 86). Then understand that you are unlikely to be expected to read every word of every publication mentioned in lectures or included in reading lists. What is needed is concentration during hours of study and the use of appropriate reading techniques: scanning, skimming, and a slow critical reading of selected passages. Rapid reading, although useful for some purposes, is not essential. On the contrary, slow reading is part of active study; and slower reading than usual is also to be expected at the start of a course when you may be acquiring additional vocabulary and being introduced to new concepts.

Do not worry if you think that your memory is not as good as that of other students, or that you are not as intelligent. In fact, most people can remember things in which they are interested and both coursework and examinations are more than a test of memory. Also, it is not easy to assess another person's intelligence. Remember that many students compensate for weaknesses at the start of a course because they are intelligent enough to accept that they must be well organised, work hard, and study effectively.

Satisfaction is derived from overcoming initial difficulties, and persevering through difficult periods, at the end of which you may see connections and things may fall into place. In this respect, studying is like climbing a hill: an all-round view cannot be expected until you reach the top.

Another fact of student life is that the students who enter a course with the best marks in qualifying examinations are not necessarily those who achieve the highest grades at college. Remember this not only if you encounter initial difficulties but also if you do not.

If you feel that the work is not sufficiently demanding or that some subjects seem boring, remember that the set work (assignments or homework) is not all that you should be doing. You must extend yourself: see that you are playing your part in trying to develop an active interest in the work. Otherwise you will find that insufficient application will result in under-achievement.

If, soon after starting a course of study, you find the work uninteresting, or not what you expected, or much too difficult, then perhaps you should be doing something else instead. However, do not give up too easily. Talk to your academic adviser or personal tutor, who will have known other students with similar problems and may reassure you or offer advice. If you wish to change to another course there will be a time limit for doing so. Obviously, it is best if you miss no classes (see Figure 5.1) and the beginning of a course is especially important. The later you join a class the harder it will be to fit in and to cope with the work.

Asking for help with study problems

If you encounter a difficulty in your studies, *first try to sort things out for yourself*. For example, think about the problem, look at your lecture notes on the subject and at appropriate parts of text-books and other sources of information. Ask other students to see if they can explain. Take opportunities to ask questions in class, particularly in tutorials and practical classes.

Most lecturers ask for questions in the last minutes of a lecture, and are pleased to speak to students privately immediately after a class – either to deal with any minor difficulty quickly or to arrange an appointment at a mutually convenient time. Similarly, other members of the academic staff are likely to be available for consultation in their office during normal working hours. With experience you will find when is the best time to call or, if necessary, how to make an appointment. You should feel able to ask your academic adviser or tutor, or any other member of the academic staff whom you find helpful and sympathetic, for help with any study problem, or with any personal problem that could stand in the way of effective study.

KEEPING FIT FOR STUDY

You will study most effectively, and derive most pleasure from your work and recreation, if you are in good health, relaxed, self-confident, and free from worry. On the one hand, anxiety about study or about personal problems, and mis-use of leisure time, interfere with study and are common causes of failure or under-achievement. On the other hand, success at college depends upon intelligence, hard work, the use of effective study, revision and examination techniques, and good health – which largely depends upon taking regular exercise, having an adequate diet, getting enough sleep, and developing good personal relationships.

Exercise and health

If you live near enough, take exercise every day by walking or cycling to college. Try to allocate time, every week, to longer walks or to more active exercise such as running, swimming or a sport. Your body is used more fully during exercise than when you are resting. In swimming, for example, your leg and arm muscles are used repeatedly, you breathe faster and deeper, and your heart beats faster than when you are inactive. Exercise contributes to a state of readiness to act in all your muscles, and after exercise you are more alert. You have a feeling of well-being and are refreshed (Figure 2.1).

Exercise is important throughout life, because it contributes to physical fitness and to mental alertness, but it is especially

WHAT, IS THIS LIFE FULL OF CARE?

Figure 2.1 Recreation, like work, is most satisfying if it provides a change and a challenge, and is enjoyable.

important while you are a student. Without exercise, preferably in
the open air, you may become lethargic, spending too much time
sitting – in lectures, in a library, and during hours of private study.
You are most likely to become lethargic in the weeks before an
examination when revision is important and you may feel that you
have no time for recreation. But this is one time when you need
exercise every day to help you remain mentally alert.

Food and health

Eating regular meals, including a variety of foods, contributes to
good health. Breakfast, after about eight hours without food, is a
most important meal which should give you a good start to the day.
But take care not to eat too much at lunch or you will be sleepy in
lectures when you want to be alert; and over-eating in the evening
may make concentration difficult during hours of study and then
make sleep more difficult at night.

Sleep and health

Anyone over the age of eighteen needs about eight hours sleep at
night. Working late into the night may be necessary from time to
time, and talking into the early hours may be an occasional pleasure, but even one late night will affect your work on the next day.
As a student, therefore, it is a good idea to get into the habit of going
to bed by eleven so that you are ready to get up at seven. This
is especially important in the weeks preceding an examination
when you must be well organized – with regular times for study,
recreation and sleep.

At the end of an evening's study, try to relax before going to bed.
A short walk in the open air can be very refreshing. Conversation or
light reading, which help you to think about other subjects, will
provide a change after study. A hot drink will help you to relax.

Friendship

It is best to be alone when you need to concentrate, but to avoid
isolation at other times. One advantage of being a full-time student,
living in college, is that you can share accommodation with students
who are studying different subjects. They will share your interest in

study – and most students choose to work at the same times (for example, early in the evening on week days). Then, in coffee breaks and over meals, you have the opportunity to broaden your interests and to talk about other things than work. Also, having friends with different interests will add interest and variety to your own life.

Plan to take an active part in student life by participating in some of the activities organised by student clubs and societies. Look at notice boards so that you are aware of what is going on in college and in town. Seek relaxation and entertainment that will take your mind away from study. For example, go to concerts or to the theatre. By following your own interests and by developing new ones, you can broaden your horizons. Make a point of doing different things which will help you to meet different people, but do not attempt too much (see page 40).

If you find study tiring and unsatisfying perhaps this is because you are bored – as a result of devoting too many hours to work or studying ineffectively in other ways, or as a result of not bothering to take an active part in college or town life. Unfortunately, many students do not achieve grades that are a true reflection of their ability, and many fail in examinations, because their studies are adversely affected by anxieties and other causes of ill health. Although these affect study they may be due not to study problems but to personal problems that are the result of a failure to use leisure time effectively.

Being yourself

If you left school recently and living away from home for the first time, you will probably have more freedom than previously to do as you like. You have an opportunity to be yourself and to influence the way your personality develops. Your student days should be a time when your self-confidence and self-reliance increase. But there is in most people a desire to conform, and soon after arriving at college, if not before, some students begin to dress as if they wished to be recognised as students. They may also be tempted, with the restrictions of home life removed, to seek new experiences.

Some students abandon their studies, and some under-achieve for reasons that have nothing to do with their academic ability. In particular, there is much concern (expressed by parents and others) about the use of drugs by young people. And much money is spent

by governments on aspects of health education. Clearly, to be effective as a student and achieve grades that are a true reflection of your
ability, you need to be in control of your life.

You will probably have read basic advice about the use of medicines and other drugs, and about other aspects of health education,
in health education leaflets and in the instructions provided with the
medicines prescribed by a doctor. Following this advice should help
you to keep fit for study:

1 Whereas a medicine containing a carefully measured amount of
  a drug may cure an illness, most drugs have side-effects and all
  drugs can be harmful if not taken exactly as instructed.
2 Even if you feel unwell, it is unwise to accept medicines
  prescribed for someone else.
3 It can be dangerous to exceed the recommended dose of any
  medicine, or to take more than one kind of medicine on the same
  day – unless your doctor has confirmed that it is safe to do so.
4 Alcohol, nicotine from cigarettes, and many other drugs are
  known to be damaging to the unborn child – and most damage
  is done in the early days of a pregnancy – when the pregnancy
  has not yet been confirmed.
5 Antihistamines taken when suffering from hay fewer may cause
  drowsiness, making concentration difficult. This is unfortunate
  if you are trying to study but is dangerous if you are driving a car
  or handling machinery.
6 Sleeping pills depress the brain and – on the next day – students
  who take them are less fit for study, or other work, or for driving
  a car than they would otherwise be. So try to keep up-to-date
  with your studies and get enough relaxation, especially just
  before going to bed. If you feel refreshed and free from worry,
  and have regular sleeping habits, you should not need sleeping
  pills.
7 If you seem to take a long time in going to sleep, try to relax so
  that you can at least benefit from the rest. Let all your muscles
  relax. Some experts suggest that it is best to think only about
  relaxing. Alternatively, to take your thoughts away from any
  current worry, you may prefer to recollect some pleasant
  experience.
8 Pep pills stimulate the brain and some people take them to overcome a feeling of tiredness, when they should be trying to relax

and go to sleep. It is unwise to take pep pills, when you have already studied for long enough, to help you to stay awake and work longer. Extreme physical tiredness and mental depression may be felt when the effects of the pills wear off, so that they have the opposite to the intended effect. There may then be a temptation to take more pep pills to help overcome the feeling of exhaustion resulting from the previous dose. This is a vicious circle. It is best to plan your week so that you are wide awake all day and ready to sleep at bed-time.

9 Nicotine, the drug in tobacco, is addictive. This is why people who smoke find it difficult to stop – even if they accept that the habit is damaging to their health and that their money would be better spent on other things. However, those who never start smoking do not have the problem of how to stop. Breathing smoke-laden air, which is called passive smoking, is a source of discomfort to non-smokers and it can also damage their health. Fortunately, smoking is usually forbidden in most college buildings, because of the risk of fire and the requirements of insurers. Non-smokers should therefore be able to work in a smoke-free atmosphere.

10 For a student, drinking alcohol regularly is likely to take up much time that would be better spent in other ways, and to be

YOU TOO COULD HAVE A BODY LIKE MINE

Figure 2.2 At college emulate the successful student, not one with his sights set on failure.

the cause of financial and other worries. Therefore, do not be impressed by the talk of the regular drinker (see Figure 2.2).

Alcohol affects the brain; and its immediate effects are more marked on those who are not used to the drug than on regular drinkers. It is not a stimulant but a depressant, which adversely affects concentration, removes inhibitions, and increases the risk of accidents. Under the influence of alcohol people are less able to exercise self control and may say and do things that they afterwards regret – perhaps for the rest of their lives. For example, a girl who does not wish to have a baby may be made pregnant by a man whom she would not have chosen as the father of her child; and a man may make pregnant a woman whom he would not have chosen as the mother of his child.

11 Some other forms of drug taking, like drinking alcohol and smoking tobacco, are part of group behaviour. Such drug taking is encouraged by those who are already addicted to the drug, and by those who profit by making and selling the drug.

Anyone who starts taking a drug may soon become addicted to it. As with all bad habits, it is better not to start drug taking than to suffer the physical and emotional harm caused by the drug and to have the problem of trying to break the addiction. It is best, therefore, to refuse any drug that is offered. Apart from other considerations, drugs that come from unreliable sources (because their manufacture and distribution is against the law) are not available in carefully measured doses and their purity is not guaranteed. Their effects are unpredictable and they may well be dangerous. If such drugs are offered by so-called friends you would be well advised to find new friends, who share your values, and to continue being yourself.

Personal relationships

In all religions people are asked to respect one another, and each person needs moral values that will help to give stability and purpose to life. Parents may exert a good influence, helping their children to tell right from wrong, but in adolescence young people accept full responsibility for their own actions. In learning to live and work with others, they establish their own code of conduct – to exercise self control, to maintain self-respect, and to show consideration for other people.

Difficulties in personal relationships, which may interfere with study plans and make concentration difficult, are most likely to be the result of romantic attachments. Indeed, the untimely end of a close friendship may cause disappointment and unhappiness, affecting course work adversely and resulting in under-achievement in examinations.

An unplanned pregnancy is likely to be even more disturbing – not only for its immediate adverse effects of study but also for the rest of one's life. Unless you want to have children, therefore, use an effective method of contraception or avoid sexual intercourse.

Everyone should be aware of the world-wide upsurge in venereal diseases, especially among young people, as a result of the greater sexual freedom made possible by the development of effective methods of contraception. These sexually transmitted diseases are caught by those who give opportunities for sexual intercourse and by those who take these opportunities. Those who are willing to have sexual encounters (heterosexual or homosexual) with people they do not know very well, have probably had similar casual encounters with other people. Even if clean and apparently healthy, they may have one of these diseases.

It takes some time for symptoms to develop, and during this time an infected person may pass on the disease. If you ever think you could have caught a venereal disease, go to see a doctor at once, without waiting for symptoms to develop. Otherwise permanent damage may result before the treatment starts. Without treatment, gonorrhoea causes pain and may make a man or woman sterile. Without treatment, syphilis may be followed, years later, by heart disease, blindness, madness and paralysis. HIV and AIDS, for which there is no cure, is likely to result in death within ten years of infection. At all stages of infection these diseases may be passed on to others and a pregnant woman may infect her child.

Coping with personal problems

It is easier to avoid difficult situations, or to cope with them, if you have clear long-term objectives and have considered how different courses of action (for example, in relation to drugs and sex) could affect your chances of attaining them. Having decided what you want to do with your life, both as a student and after leaving college, you are prepared if anyone tries to persuade you to do anything against your will.

You are entitled to your own opinions as to what is right and wrong, and should be prepared to stand up for yourself. It is best to stick to your principles and not lower your self-imposed standards to conform with what appears to be the behaviour of the majority, or with what you think are the opinions of the majority. You can maintain your self-respect, and the respect of most other people, if you have the strength of character to do what you consider to be right in any situation.

Although, if you have problems, they are likely to be similar to those encountered by other students, you will need to consult other sources for more specific and more detailed information than can be given in a book such as this. Also, if you have difficulty in finding the answer to a question, or the solution to any problem, do not be afraid to ask for help. Especially when you are new at college, you may need advice and the people you would previously have consulted may not be readily available. You may not know where to turn for help. This is why you have an academic adviser or personal tutor who, if unable to help directly, may suggest that you should see another member of the academic staff, or help you to make an appointment to see a member of the student advisory services (such as a students' counsellor or careers officer, or a member of the student health services).

If you have any personal problem, by all means try to think of a satisfactory solution. It is usually a good idea to sleep on a problem: things may seem different in the morning. But do not brood on things for too long. Writing a letter home or talking over any problem with a sympathetic listener – a parent, a tutor, a friend – may help in itself. The sooner you either find a solution or decide that you just have to accept things as they are, the sooner your worries may be removed or relieved, leaving you free to concentrate on your studies.

3

Make good use of your time

At school, time is allocated to organised classes, including recreation periods, and perhaps also to private study. Teachers set definite tasks for homework. Pupils may be able to learn all they need to know about a subject from one teacher and one textbook; and they may be told exactly what they must know for an examination.

At college some of your time is still organised for you. You are expected to attend lectures, tutorials, seminars, practical classes, field trips, and other educational visits; and some tasks are set for homework. There are no time-tabled periods for games, athletics or physical training, but the facilities are there if you wish to use them. Also, there are many clubs and societies that you could join. Therefore, unless you are well organised you could easily devote too little or too much time to study, or too much to procrastination.

ACCEPT RESPONSIBILITY FOR YOUR LEARNING

The last years at school are a period of transition. Senior pupils should need less help than previously and should be accepting more responsibility for their own progress – as they learn to be students. The poor performance of some students at college is the result of their failure to take the initiative (see Figure 1.4, page 8).

At school it is the teacher's job to capture and hold the pupil's interest. A teacher asks questions to make everyone think, to check that they understand, and to revise previous work. But at college a lecturer's task is to stimulate your thinking and help you to know what to study. It is up to you to ask questions when necessary. Learning is your responsibility. You are unlikely to be told exactly what is expected of a good student, but you can benefit from the comments of different lecturers, from advice in course, year and module guides, and from reading books on study skills. Be prepared to consider ideas and advice from many sources and to assess your own progress.

After school, on a more advanced course, the work should be more demanding. A higher standard is expected and a different approach. Study is interesting and rewarding – but it *is* work. Your success as a student, as in your career, will depend upon your interest and enthusiasm (motivation); your ability to think, understand, select, organise, remember, and explain; and upon how hard you work, how effectively you work, and how effectively you use your leisure time. It is not possible to place these things in order of importance (see Figure 3.1). However, note that although by hard work you can compensate for deficiencies in other respects, you can make your work much easier by good organisation – so that you make effective use of your study and leisure time.

When you start organised classes you will probably be given a course guide containing: (a) the names of academic staff responsible for each part of the course and details of how they can be contacted, (b) a time-table, and (c) a syllabus indicating the course content (what you will be taught or what you should study) or a list of learning outcomes (things you should know, understand, or be able to do, by the end of the course). You may also be given a shorter guide at the start of each year, and an even shorter outline at the start of each aspect, module or unit of the course.

From the information available at the start, prepare a course plan – including the times and titles of your lecture courses, practical work, field studies, project work, tests and examinations, and vacations. Referring to this plan will help you: (a) to see at a glance how your work at any time fits in to the course as a whole, (b) to be well organised, and (c) to remain in control. However, study is not the only activity in a student's life: you also contribute to and benefit from college life. In college clubs and societies, in addition to being with friends who have similar interests to your own, you may be able to gain valuable experience of committee work, of speaking in public, and (if you wish) of the duties of a club secretary or

Figure 3.1 Some factors that influence performance. The marks and grades awarded are not just an indication of ability. Students also differ in their starting point (influenced by their home background and previous education), in their motivation, and in their use of time.

chairman. In both academic and non-academic activities you gain experience of getting along well with people and developing good working relationships and friendships based upon mutual respect and understanding.

You may have other commitments, especially if you live at home, and there will be attractions in the town. You will not, therefore, have time to do all those things that you might like to do. It is important to consider this at the start of your course so that you can *have a social life that does not take up too much of your time.*

Non-academic interests contribute to personal development: without them you are likely to become narrow-minded and dull. Furthermore, when you come to look for employment, both your academic achievements and your non-academic interests will indicate to an employer the kind of person you are.

To do well at college most students have to exercise self-discipline, and the qualification obtained is more than a measure of ability (see Figure 3.1). Your success at one kind of work (being a student) may be taken as an indication of your ability to tackle another (as an employee). This is especially important if you change your mind about what you would like to do after leaving college, or if you are unable to obtain employment in your chosen career. Most employers are looking for employees with a variety of interests who have more to offer than a paper qualification.

By planning your course, year by year and week by week, you can keep a sensible balance between academic and non-academic interests. You can plan not just your studies but the whole of your student life. On the one hand you will not want to feel a slave to a rigid timetable; but, on the other hand, if you fall behind with your studies you will have to work even harder than usual to catch up. It is best to *organise your timetable to suit yourself*, so that you can work more effectively and have more leisure time than would otherwise be possible. If you think that you have so much to do that you have no time to spend on planning, be assured that your timetable will enable you to use your time more effectively and so save time later.

Many students who do not organise their time effectively, and do not communicate very well in writing, nevertheless manage to pass their examinations. In this sense they are successful, but it is not possible to know how much more successful they might have been had they used better study, revision and examination techniques. Nor can we know how many of those who fail might have passed if they had worked more effectively and been better able to display their knowledge in examinations. We know only the grade obtained, not what might have been.

ORGANISE YOUR YEAR

Your purpose, as a student, should be to master all your subjects. To do this it is necessary to work steadily throughout the year, not just in the last few weeks before your examinations. Keep up-to-date with course work, week by week, so that you have time to think about each subject, to undertake background reading, and to learn as you go along.

If your days and weeks are well organised, you should be up-to-date with your studies at the end of each week and, therefore, at the end of each term. You can then use each vacation, depending upon its length, as an opportunity for a short break from your studies –

for a few days in a short vacation or for two or three weeks in a long vacation. But remember that college vacations are not intended to be holidays. Nor should they be devoted entirely to paid employment.

If you are studying full-time, you will spend a little more than half of each year at college. In vacations, therefore, allocate many hours to active study to keep each subject alive in your mind and to build on the foundations laid at college. Keep your long-term objective in view, and do not waste time. Without planning at the start of each vacation, and exercising self-discipline every day, you may find that the time slips away and you achieve little or nothing. You can easily lose an hour by getting up late, then lose another reading a newspaper or magazine after breakfast, and so on. Whether you are studying full-time or part-time, be positive: regard each vacation as *an opportunity for revision, consolidation, and background reading*, as well as for recreation, so that you come to feel that you know your subjects and are well prepared for the next term's work (see Table 3.1).

Table 3.1 First year studies at college and in vacations

Term 1	Organised for you	Student centred learning
(11 weeks)	Organised classes	Keeping up-to-date with course work and completing other necessary studies
	3 weeks vacation	Revision of first term's work
Term 2		
	Mid-sessional test or Semester 1 Examinations	Keeping up-to-date with course work and completing other necessary studies
Term 3		
	Organised classes completed Examinations	Final revision for First year (Semester 2) examinations
	12 weeks vacation	Holiday (2 weeks) Private study and recreation Consolidation and background reading Preparation for second year's work Holiday (1 Week)

ORGANISE YOUR WEEK

At the start of each term, prepare a timetable or schedule that includes all your organised classes and the times that you intend to devote to private study. These things should come first in your order of priorities. Then include any other commitments and take care to leave enough time for recreation (see Tables 3.2–3.4) and for sleep. Note that there are 168 hours in each week and consider how you will use them. You *should* spend 56 hours asleep, and you *could* devote 56 hours to study – which would leave 56 hours for recreation and other essential activities.

A full-time student who is at college for eight hours each day, and allows one hour for lunch, can work for 35 hours each week – and would need to study for another 14 hours each week (in the evenings and at week-ends) to make a 49-hour working week. This means, in term time, that a student of science or engineering, with 24 hours of organised classes, could devote 25 hours to private study; and an arts student, with 12 hours of organised classes could devote 37 hours to private study.

A part-time student who is engaged in other work for seven hours on each week day, and who has three hours of organised classes on each of two evenings, will need to allocate eight hours to private study to make a 49-hour working week. Part-time study is not easy (see page 198), but some of the subjects studied may be directly relevant to the student's paid employment and others may provide a complete change from other work, and so may offer, in themselves, absorbing interests and opportunities for recreation and relaxation. The part-time student may decide, therefore, to allocate more than eight hours each week to private study.

Your timetable is your schedule for work. Instead of writing the words library or study (as in Tables 3.2–3.4) decide which subjects you will study in each private study session – so that you can allocate enough time to each of your subjects. Make your plan and modify it in the light of experience; then do your best to stick to it, so that it is more than a statement of your good intentions. As far as possible, devote the same times each week to the same subjects so that you can prepare for classes, check your notes after classes, write laboratory reports promptly etc. *You will not* then make the mistake of devoting too much time to your favourite subjects at the

Table 3.2 Timetable (schedule) of a student in the first year of a two-year Diploma course in Business Studies*

	M	T	W	T	F	S	S
1	S BO	S BE	L Mk	L BO	L DP	Study xxxxxxxxx	
2	S BO xxxxxxxxx	S BE	L Mk	L CL	L DP xxxxxxxxx	Study	
3	Library	L BE xxxxxxxxx	S Mk	S BT	Library		
4	Library	Library	S CL	S BT	Library		
1	L BT	Library xxxxxxxxx		L CL xxxxxxxxx	Library		
2		GA		Library	Library xxxxxxxxx xxxxxxxxx		
3	S DP	GA		Library xxxxxxxxx	Library		
4				Library			
1	Study xxxxxxxxx		Study xxxxxxxxx	Study xxxxxxxxx			Study xxxxxxxxx
2	Study		Study	Study			Study
3							

Key

L = Lecture	BO = Business organisation	CL = Consumer law
S = Seminar	BE = Business environment	DP = Data processing
xxxxx = Break	BT = Business techniques	Mk = Marketing
	GA = Group assignment	

* Note. This student has organised classes for 20 hours each week and devotes 20 hours to private study: a well-motivated student would probably do more.

Table 3.3 Timetable (schedule) of a student in the second year of a Combined Arts Degree course with Geography and Literature as main subjects*

	M	T	W	T	F	S	S
1	Study		Library	Library	L AL		
2			Library xxxxxxxxxx	Library xxxxxxxxxx	xxxxxxxxxx L VL		
3	S AL	L VB	Library	Library	xxxxxxxxxx S VL		
4		S VB					
1	Library	L WE					
2	Library xxxxxxxxxx	S WE xxxxxxxxxx	Library				
3	Library	L DS	Library xxxxxxxxxx	L WR			Study
4		S DS	Library	L WR			Study
1	Study	Study	Study	Study			
2	Study xxxxxxxxxx	Study xxxxxxxxxx	Study xxxxxxxxxx	Study xxxxxxxxxx			
3	Study	Study	Study	Study			

Key

L = Lecture	AL = American Literature	DS = Development and Society
S = Seminar	VL = Victorian Literature	WE = Western Europe
xxxxx = Break	VB = Legacy of Victorian Britain	WR = Water Resources

* *Note.* This student has only 12 hours of organised classes and clearly could achieve a better balance between work and recreation, and yet devote more time to private study. Too much time is allocated to study on some days and not enough on others.

> Tables 3.2 to 3.4 are the timetables of three full-time students. Look at them to see how these students allocate their time. Read the footnotes to the tables; and then look again at your own timetable. Are you making effective use of your time?

expense of weaker subjects, on which you should probably be spending more of your time.

Plan ahead as far as you can so that you keep up-to-date in all subjects and hand in set work on time (see Table 3.5, page 33). However, do not make the common mistake of thinking that your set work is all that you need to do. Being a student means that *you make* the decisions about what needs to be done: you should be doing more than is demanded.

Behave as if you were employed in one of the professions and stick to *self-imposed* hours of work. On weekdays, if you have no organised class, *make an early start in the library* and plan to make good use of free periods during the day. These are not times when you should be doing nothing: they are opportunities for study or for recreation. Do not spend more than ten to fifteen minutes, regularly, on tea or coffee breaks. Otherwise you will find that hours slip away.

If you expect to have an hour free during the day, there is time to find a quiet spot, complete forty minutes of effective study, and then walk to your next class. You may think that not much can be achieved in forty minutes but this is more time than you would be allowed in an examination for thinking about a question, planning and writing your answer, and checking your work. There are many kinds of tasks that can be completed in less than an hour (see page 34), providing only that you avoid distractions and know exactly what you want to achieve in the time. Some of your study sessions, during the day, will be longer than forty minutes; in these you can do more.

On week days, when you study in the evening, it is probably better to devote three hours to study and one to recreation than to try to work for four hours. You could not achieve twice as much in four hours as you could in two; and you will probably achieve little more in four hours than you could in three. At weekends it is probably best to study in one, two or three-hour sessions, to ensure that you have longer periods for recreation, and to give some thought to your next week's work.

Table 3.4 Timetable (schedule) of a student in the final year of a Degree course in Electrical and Electronic Engineering*

	M	T	W	T	F	S	S
1	Project	L Net xxxxxxxxxx	L MSD xxxxxxxxxx	Study	Lab		
2	Project	L Com	S MSD		Lab		
3	xxxxxxxxxx Project	xxxxxxxxxx Library	xxxxxxxxxx Library	L Net	xxxxxxxxxx Lab		
4	Project	xxxxxxxxxx Library	Library	Library	Library		
1	Project	L Man xxxxxxxxxx	L Com xxxxxxxxxx	L Con xxxxxxxxxx	S		
2	Project	S Man	L Elec xxxxxxxxxx	S Con	S		
3	Project		S Elec xxxxxxxxxx	Study	Project		
4	Study	Study	Study				
1	Study	Study	Study	Study	Study		
2	Study	Study	Study	Study	Study		
3							

Key
L = Lecture	Net = Network	Elec = Electronic engineering
S = Seminar	Com = Communication	Con = Control
Lab = Practical class	Man = Management	MSD = Microprocessor System
xxxxx = Break		Design

* *Note.* This student might be well advised to take a break earlier in the week (perhaps on Wednesday evening) and to study for at least three hours at the week-end in this final year.

Table 3.5 Answering a question in course work

Tasks		Activities	Minutes	Count down
1	Work set on Monday	Thinking		
2	Monday evening	Planning	30	7
3	Tuesday morning	Searching	40	6
4	Wednesday evening	Reading	30	5
	Thursday			4
5	Friday morning	Revising plan	10	3
6		Writing	30	
	Saturday			2
7	Sunday morning	Checking	10	1
	Monday			0
			Total* 150	

* Note   In course work two-and-a-half hours could be well spent on a composition that in an examination would have to be completed in a much shorter time

Try to arrange regular times that you will spend with friends, in different activities, so that they know when you are studying – and that you will not want to be disturbed at these times.

By working to a timetable you can ensure that you do devote enough time to study and enough to recreation. Then, by organising your days, you can plan to use each study period effectively. In this way you will do enough work without over-working.

ORGANISE YOUR DAY

Allocate some time to going over class work, while it is fresh in your mind, to make sure that your notes are clear and correct. Check that you will be able to understand them later but do not get into the time-wasting habit of copying out notes just to make them neater.

Devote some time to regular revision (see page 68) and to thinking about each subject, with your lecture notes as a guide to what is required. Spend enough time on learning and on background reading. If you have been given an outline of the course, in which the topics to be considered each week are listed, spend some time at the week-ends on preliminary reading. Allocate some of your time to preparing for practical classes, seminars and tutorials, so that you are better able to understand your work and to contribute to discussions.

Before you finish work each day, clear your working surface. Consider what you have achieved and look at your timetable or work-plan for the next day.

1 Make a list of any engagements or other things that you must do.
2 List a limited number of study tasks that you expect to complete.
3 Decide how you will use any free periods during the day.
4 Put together any books, papers or other materials that you will need.

Some people find it helpful to use personal organiser software on a personal computer to help them organise their time, but all that most people need is a job list – which can be on the back of an envelope that is always kept to hand, can be up-dated as necessary during the day, and should be replaced with a new list at the end of each day's work.

You must have a particular piece of work in mind for each study session, so that you know not only what you will do but also when and where. You can then complete tasks in order of priority, avoid distractions (such as conversation or the temptation to tackle some less urgent but more intriguing problem), and concentrate on one thing at a time. You will not then waste time, when you sit down to work, wondering what to do next (see Figure 1.3, page 7).

Listing tasks is a matter of accepting that you cannot do all the things that you might like to be doing, recognising what needs to be done, and establishing an order of priority. Here is the difference between a pupil who has to be told what to do and a student who can see what needs to be done. For example, a student will still be given clearly defined pieces of homework but within each of these it is possible to recognise smaller tasks.

1 Think, and prepare notes of ideas and information that must be included in your answer (see page 71).
2 Prepare a topic outline for your answer (see page 72).
3 Fill gaps in your knowledge (see page 75) and, if necessary . . .
4 Undertake background reading to get additional ideas.
5 Revise your topic outline, and . . .
6 Write your answer (see page 119).
7 Check and, if necessary, revise your work (see page 124).

Allocate time to each of these tasks (see Table 3.5) and try to ensure that each task is one that can be completed in this time. Recognizing what needs to be done enables you to organise your studies and to do the best work of which you are capable in the time available.

This positive approach to your studies means, even in dealing with set work, that you are in control. You make the decisions, and have no need to worry about the possibility that you may not complete the work satisfactorily and on time. Instead of struggling to cope as you go along, it pays to plan ahead. Such anticipation will increase your self-confidence and help you to provide a basis for effective learning.

As you work on your notes you may recognise gaps in your knowledge and understanding, and these can be noted as things that need your further attention.

> Look up the name of . . . or the title of the book by . . .
> Find out more about . . .
> Read chapter . . . of textbook on . . . before lecture on . . .

Keep to your timetable each day but be prepared to renumber tasks in your list of things to do, to revise your order of priority when necessary, so that you can concentrate on the most important or most urgent tasks *one at a time*. If you do not complete any task in the time that you had allocated to it, look at your list when you prepare for your next day's work. Uncompleted tasks can then be carried forward and not forgotten. Working to a timetable, and with a list of things to do, does not mean being inflexible. At times some subjects will require more attention than others, and some tasks will take longer than you expected.

Your numbered list of *things to do* helps you to organise your day. Crossing off each task as it is completed is a source of satisfaction and an indication that you are making progress; and

adding a task to the list, so that you will not forget it, leaves you free
to concentrate on a higher task in your order of priority.

CONCENTRATE DURING HOURS OF STUDY

If you have difficulty in concentrating during hours of study, here
are some basic rules that will help you to improve your study habits.
(See also Figure 3.2.)

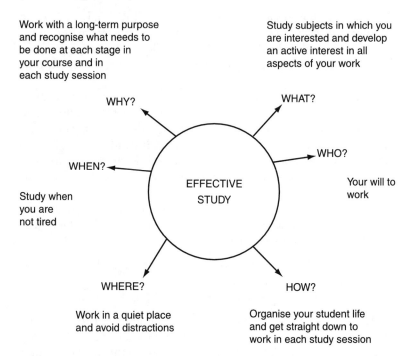

Work with a long-term purpose
and recognise what needs to
be done at each stage in
your course and in
each study session

Study subjects in which you
are interested and develop
an active interest in all
aspects of your work

WHY?   WHAT?

WHEN?   WHO?

EFFECTIVE
STUDY

Your will to
work

Study when
you are
not tired

WHERE?   HOW?

Work in a quiet place
and avoid distractions

Organise your student life
and get straight down to
work in each study session

Figure 3.2 Factors that contribute to motivation – your will to work –
which is the basis for effective study.

1 Having prepared a timetable, *start each study session on time.*
2 *Try to study* in a quiet part of a library, in an empty classroom,
  or in your own room, *where you expect to be free from distractions* and interruptions.
3 *Make good use of study facilities in a library*: the atmosphere
  should be conducive to study. Also, it is a good idea to study
  regularly where other people are working because this should

help you to concentrate and give you practice in working under something like examination conditions.

4 *Maintain a good posture* so that you can sit comfortably during long periods of active study. Sit upright and try to ensure that your chair and working surface are the right height for you (see Figure 8.1, page 111).

5 *Make sure that you have enough space* for your notes and other necessary books or papers (see Figure 3.3). Some people get used to working amidst a familiar jumble, but you are advised not to allow your working surface to become cluttered with things that are not required for the task in hand, and which can provide only distractions.

6 *Make sure that your working surface is sufficiently and evenly illuminated*; and that the light is not in your eyes. Daylight is best and, if you are right-handed, the light should come from your left (as in Figure 3.3). Adjust the light to suit your purpose: you will need more for preparing an accurate diagram than for

GET STRAIGHT DOWN TO WORK!

Figure 3.3 Avoid distractions: sit in a quiet place and keep to hand just the things you need for a particular task.

writing or reading. Do not work in intense light, and avoid glare from the working surface or from papers. For reading, support the book at an angle so that all words are about equidistant from your eyes.

If you normally read quickly but find that you are reading slowly, this may be due to fatigue. Reading critically and making notes will help you to maintain your concentration, but do not read for too long without a break. A defect of vision (or hearing) may be a great handicap for a student and it is advisable to see a doctor at once if you suspect that you may need help.

7 Before starting to study, try to *ensure that the room is well ventilated and at a suitable temperature.* You are unlikely to be able to maintain attention for long in a badly ventilated and over-heated room.

8 *Undertake problem solving, planning and other demanding tasks* and work at your weaker subjects (which you find most difficult) *when you are at your best.* This will probably be in the morning or at the start of an evening's work. Tasks that you are looking forward to, or which you expect to be straightforward, can be done in the second and third hours of an evening's study session. It is better to get up an hour earlier to study, in the morning, than to stay up an hour later at night. In the evening it is best to start work early, to finish early, and to do something different during the last hour before going to bed.

9 *Make each task an activity*, and use different strategies for learning (a) so that you are always aware of your course and of each subject as a whole as well as in parts, and (b) so that an evening's study comprises different kinds of activity.

Long term: obtaining an overview

Survey syllabus for your course on . . . to see how the part you are currently studying fits into the whole.

Look at contents pages of books on . . . to see different approaches to the subject and its scope.

Look at titles of lectures included in a particular course, to put each lecture in perspective.

Review your progress and revise regularly.

Short term: moving forward step by step
Gathering and processing information

Prepare for classes on . . .

Check notes after classes on . . .
Look up references mentioned in class on . . .
Find more information about . . .
Concentrated study
Read critically chapter . . . of . . .
Incorporate relevant points in lecture notes on . . .
Plan answer to question on . . .
Solve problems on page . . . of . . .
Write . . .
Summarise . . .

With such clearly defined tasks you know exactly what has to be done and you know when each task is complete. You will be able to sit down and get straight on with the task you have planned for this study session. Keep your mind on your work: avoid daydreaming. If you regard each task as a challenge, completing it will be a source of satisfaction. But this will be true only if each task is one that you can complete in the time you have allocated to it.

10 On completing each task, *review your work* and check for accuracy, orderliness and completeness. Consider what you have achieved and make a note of what must be done next time you study this subject. Devote a few minutes to revision. Put away the books and papers relating to this task before you start work on the next.

11 *Do not mistake boredom for fatigue.* You will find it easy to concentrate on a subject that interests you. Developing an active interest in all subjects of your course (see page 75) is therefore the basis for effective study. (See Figure 3.2, page 36).

12 *Do not work for too long at one task.* Most people concentrate best for the first twenty minutes or so. Therefore, so that you can maintain attention and avoid daydreaming, try to break your work into tasks that can be completed in under an hour (see Table 3.5). Setting a time limit also provides an incentive for you to start on time and to work steadily at each task.

13 Organise your studies so that successive tasks are *different kinds of activity*: solve, plan, check, make notes on, review, write, read, etc.

14 From time to time, *take a break of two or three minutes*. If you just stand, take a few deep breaths, exercise your arms, and walk

around the room a few times, this should help you to maintain attention when you resume work.

Towards the end of the second hour of a three-hour study session, take a 10-minute break. Move away from your work and do something different. Take such longer breaks at the end of one piece of work (as you would at the end of a lecture), so that you have the satisfaction of completing one task and can make a fresh start on the next.

The first hour of a two-hour study session may be spent as follows: 40 minutes for *study*, 10 minutes to *review* and *revise*, 5 minutes to put away your papers and prepare for the next task, and 5 minutes for a break. The second hour may comprise 40 minutes for *study*, 10 minutes to *review* and *revise* and put away your papers, and 10 minutes for a break. Then do not allow this break to last more than 10 minutes: start your third hour's study on time. You may find that some of your best ideas come to mind during short breaks in your studies, in moments of quiet relaxation and contemplation, and during recreational activities when your attention is on other things (see page 109).

15 You may have difficulty in concentrating on your studies because of some anxiety – which may or may not be connected with your studies (see Chapter 2). *Try to deal with this problem as soon as you can* so that you will be able to concentrate better on your work. Similarly, if something is demanding your attention (perhaps you have to make a telephone call or write a letter) then it is best to do this at once and quickly *before* the time you have allocated for study, so that it can be crossed off your list of things to do.

Exercising self-discipline and being well organised, with a positive approach to the course as a whole, in maintaining good study habits week by week, in allocating study periods to definite tasks, and in adopting effective study and revision techniques, will help you to avoid stress, to concentrate on your work and to achieve more than would otherwise be possible. You will also be able to relax in your leisure time. In consequence, you should find study more satisfying and recreation more enjoyable.

Some good students may seem to learn without effort and to work without a written timetable, but this is not to say that their work is unorganised. The organisation may be in their minds. They recognise, perhaps without writing a list, what needs to be done and which tasks must be done first. They have time for leisure activities but do not waste time. However, to be so well organised (or perhaps to be better organised) most students need the self-imposed discipline of keeping to a fairly rigid written timetable and the reminder provided by a list of tasks numbered in order of priority.

Part 2

Student centred learning

In lectures, for most of the time, you *listen* and make carefully selected concise notes. In other group activities, especially tutorials and practical classes, you receive more personal attention: you have opportunities to *think* about your subjects, to *observe* (find things out for yourself), and to *learn* by putting your thoughts into words – in conversations and discussions.

In private study, although working alone, you use your lecture notes as well as books and other records prepared by other people. The distinction between group activities and private study, therefore, is not clear cut. One supports the other and both provide opportunities for learning. You relate what you *read* to things you already know and develop your ability to *express yourself* first by *writing* answers to questions set as assignments in course work and later by preparing a longer composition based on a project or other special study.

Therefore, whether you are studying part-time or full-time, or by distance learning, many of your activities are *student-centred* (in contrast to a lecture when the lecturer provides the driving force). They provide full-time students with opportunities to develop the personal skills that many part-time students develop in their full time employment (see Table 1.1, page 9); and provide all students with opportunities to further develop these skills.

4

Listen and learn

In spite of the central place of the notes you make in lectures, tutorials, seminars, and other organised classes, in drawing together all aspects of your work and as an aid to learning (see Figure 7.2, page 96), and in spite of the time you devote to making and improving them, you are unlikely to be given advice on how to make notes. Furthermore, in contrast to other aspects of course work, you will not have the benefit of an assessor's comments on your notes: they are for your eyes only.

So, consider: (a) the importance of attending all organised classes, (b) the value of lectures in study, and (c) the different note-making techniques students use. Then take a critical look at your own notes to see if you can improve your note-making skills.

BEING THERE

You would be wise to look at the syllabus for your course, or at the list of learning objectives, upon which examinations should be based. But your best and only complete guide to the course content (especially when examinations are set and marked internally) is provided in the classes that you are expected to attend. Your intention, therefore, should be to attend all classes, to arrive on time, and to listen carefully to every word. There is no substitute for being there. Good students attend regularly – and those who miss classes are usually losing interest, or are over-confident, and are unlikely to achieve grades that are a true reflection of their ability.

The notes you make during organised classes are your own summary of what was said. They are of use to you not only for what is recorded but also as an aid to your memory. Looking at these notes, later, you will be able to remember much more of what was said by the lecturer. You should also have a record of the questions asked by yourself, and by other students, and of the lecturer's replies.

You cannot make up for missing a lecture by reading a book or by copying notes made by another student. Obviously, another student's notes cannot remind you of things that happened in the class that you did not attend. Also, students differ in their knowledge at the start of a class, in what they select to note, and in the way they make notes. Another student's notes may also be an incomplete record of even the lecturer's main points and they may contain mistakes and misunderstandings. If they contain the student's own comments you may be unable to distinguish the lecturer's words from the student's thoughts. If necessary therefore, after an unavoidable absence, look at another student's notes and make what you can of them. Obtain exact details of any set work. Then, after apologising for your absence, ask the lecturer how you should attempt to fill the gap in your own notes (see Figure 4.1).

THE VALUE OF LECTURES IN STUDY

Reading a book on a subject is not an alternative to attending a course of lectures on the same subject. The lecture and the textbook are complementary: they should be used in different ways.

At the start of a course of lectures you will find it helpful to copy the appropriate part of the syllabus, or the relevant learning objectives, on to the first page of your lecture notes for the course – so that you will be aware of the scope of the studies proposed. But note that the lecturer may spend more time on some aspects than on others; and may leave you to deal with some topics entirely on your own.

In the first lecture of each part of your course a good lecturer will answer your questions: why (purpose of course), what (content of course), and when (development of subject week by week). This is rather like giving you a map and a timetable for a journey, so that you will know your route, how you are progressing, and when you

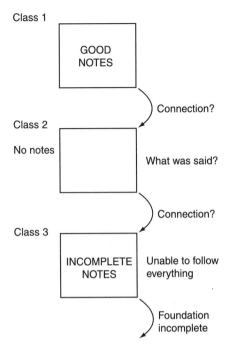

Figure 4.1 Some consequences of missing one class. You benefit less than you should from the first class; you miss the second; and you may not fully understand the third. Your foundation for further study is incomplete.

should arrive at your destination. The first lecture is therefore important, but so are the others – each of which will probably be devoted to one aspect of the subject. And the last lecture, in which no new ground may be covered, is a summing up that no student can afford to miss.

You will find it helpful to have a list of the topics to be considered in each week of the course, with suggestions for preliminary reading. However, some lecturers prefer to say, at the end of each lecture, what the next one will be about. In a well planned course the lecturer acts as a pace setter. Attending classes, therefore, should help you to move smoothly through the course and to complete the necessary studies in time for your examinations. Being there helps you to know what the lecturer considers to be the most important points for you in this course. Listening to the lecture, and participating in any discussion, helps you to think about your subject and to move forward in an organised way – faster than would be possible if you worked alone.

Listening to a lecture, *looking* at words written on a blackboard or at other visual aids, *taking a critical interest*, and *recording* carefully *selected* and well *organised* notes, are all *aids to active study*. These activities help you to maintain attention, to pick out key ideas, to recognise an orderly pattern in what is being said, to learn, and to remember.

Creative thinking is aided by concentrating on main points, concepts and ideas, rather than detail. *Learning is aided* by the use of different senses: you see and hear, and you feel the pen moving in your hand as you repeat (by writing or drawing) those things that you consider most important. *This repetition helps you to remember.* For all these reasons, attending lectures regularly and making good notes is probably the most effective study technique for introducing new material and developing your interest. You absorb the most ideas and information for the least work, and you are well placed to continue your studies.

Do not lose interest in a lecture if you think that you have heard it all before. If you have done some preliminary reading you will expect to be on familiar ground. This should help you to appreciate the lecturer's approach; to select and note, particularly, anything that is not sufficiently explained in your textbook; to appreciate nuances, recognise differences of opinion, follow arguments, understand conclusions, and so learn more than would otherwise have been possible. Going over things again should help to clear up any misunderstandings and to fix important points in your mind. You should also be well placed to ask questions if anything remains unclear.

The lecturer should neither teach the subject, in the sense of telling you all that you need to know, nor provide a summary of your textbook. The lecturer should:

1 Guide your thoughts.
2 Indicate the scope of the subject.
3 Provide a level of treatment that is appropriate to your needs.
4 Emphasise basic essentials.
5 Explain difficult points.
6 Clarify aspects that are commonly misunderstood.
7 Give evidence and examples.

8 Draw attention to different interpretations of the evidence.
9 Relate new work to your previous knowledge and experience.
10 Suggest sources of further information and ideas.
11 Stimulate your thinking.
12 Help you to develop a critical interest in the subject.
13 Answer your questions.

In lectures it is best to sit in the middle and near the front, with other keen students, where you are close to the lecturer, can hear all that is said, see any visual aids clearly, and feel closely involved. In this position you will not be distracted by other students, sitting between you and the lecturer.

MAKE NOTES AS YOU LISTEN

In a lecture to a large number of students, a lecturer may neither ask questions nor wish to answer questions – except at the end. However, communication should not be one way: as a student you should not be passive. You are participating in a group activity. A good lecturer, who is sensitive to the needs and reactions of the audience, will look around the room and try to maintain eye contact with everyone. You can help by looking at the lecturer and, by your facial expression, *showing that you are interested* and that you do or do not understand. If necessary, the lecturer will respond by repeating, by putting things in a different way, or by summarising – in an attempt to ensure that your attention is maintained and that you do understand.

The worst lectures are those in which the lecturer reads notes and most students try to record every word: the lecturer's notes are transferred to the notepaper of the students. The students have difficulty in keeping up, are likely to make mistakes, and nobody has time to think. Alternatively, the bad lecturer uses visual aids to display such things as proofs and classical derivations which are written out in full in the textbooks for the course. Again, most students are so busy recording that they are unable to concentrate on the argument. As a result, they miss important comments and necessary explanations and are unable to understand. They are not ready to ask questions either during the argument, when something is not clear, or at the end when things are still not clear.

A good lecturer provides a list of titles, with the date of each lecture, at the start of the lecture course; then states the title at the start of each lecture. The purpose of the lecture should be clear from the title and from the lecturer's introductory remarks. You should be able to see how one lecture follows on from previous lectures and is leading to the next. Is the lecturer explaining different points of view, introducing new ideas, adding information, presenting evidence, or drawing conclusions?

You should be aware of the lecturer's purpose and should be listening, thinking and anticipating. You should be relating what is being said to what you already know, and selecting points so that your notes are a digest. Instead of *taking notes* dictated by the lecturer, you should be listening, selecting and *making your own notes*. The lecturer may help you to select and record the main points by writing headings and key words on a board, by repetition, a change of voice, a meaningful pause, or by using such phrases as: *most important, note that*, and *remember that*, to emphasise things that you may wish to record. Words such as *first, second, also, furthermore, moreover, therefore*, and *finally*, indicate stages in an argument. *But* and *however* indicate a qualification. *Because* indicates a reason. *On the one hand* and *on the other hand* indicate a contrast. *Illustrated by, for example*, and *as seen in*, indicate an example. All these words, although you may not record them, help you to make good notes.

Lecture notes are so important as a record of the course content, and as a basis for further studies and for revision, that you must try to make good notes from the start of any course. If you looked at the notes taken by students who had attended a lecture, you would find that they had all selected different points for inclusion and arranged them in different ways. This is as it should be. There is no one correct method for making notes. However, consider the following suggestions.

You have to look down from time to time to make brief notes but try not to write non-stop. You can make note-taking easier by using well-known abbreviations and symbols (see Table 4.1) and, for example, by using capital initial letters instead of proper names – if this can be done without causing confusion. However, use abbreviations so that you can spend more time on listening, thinking, and selecting, not so that you can make more notes.

To record every word of every lecture, if this could be done, in shorthand for example, would be a waste of time.

Table 4.1 Some useful abbreviations and symbols

Abbreviation	Meaning	Symbol	Meaning
N.B.	note particularly	mm	millimetre(s)
cf.	compare	cm	centimetre(s)
ct.	contrast	m	metre(s)
e.g.	for example	km	kilometre(s)
i.e.	that is	ha	hectare(s)
no.	number	cm^3	cubic centimetre(s)
p.	page	l	litre(s)
pp.	pages	kg	kilogramme(s)
ch.	chapter	t	tonne(s)
ed.	edition or editor	s	second(s)
w/o	without	min	minute(s)
fig.	figure (diagram)	h	hour(s)
ref.	reference	°C	degree Celsius
C19	19th century	%	per cent
L.	Latin	+	and or plus
Gk.	Greek	=	equal to
vol.	volume	≠	different from
conc.	concentrated	<	less than
aq.	aqueous	>	greater than

1 You would not be able to take a critical interest in the lectures.
2 You would not be trying to understand and learn.
3 You would not be ready to ask questions at the end of each lecture.
4 You would have a record that was too long to be of use in your further studies.
5 You would have to read through this record, later, to pick out the essentials of each lecture, so that you could *make your own notes*. To make notes it is necessary to be selective; and you are advised to select at the first opportunity (in the lecture). You do not have time to do everything twice.

Sequential notes

Record first the title of the lecture, the name of the lecturer, and the date. Listen carefully and record all the main points in the order in which they are made during the lecture. Record:

1 A numbered list of main points (see Figure 4.2).

Main, A. **Coping with lectures**

Use
unlined or
wide-lined
A4 paper

1 **Before lecture**
Do some preliminary reading.
Arrive on time : first few minutes
are important.

LIST

MAIN

POINTS

2 **In lectures**   Think positively.
LISTEN. SELECT: what you
write matters, not how much.
Selecting and making notes is
an aid to concentration.

3 **After lecture**. REVIEW your notes.
Are they accurate, complete,
and understandable?

LEAVE
SPACE
in notes
and
in margins
for
additions
later in
lecture
and
afterwards

FILL IN ANY GAPS: Working on
your notes is an aid to under-
standing and to remembering.
NOTE In lecture, to help you select,
listen for clues. Is the lecturer
INTRODUCING? ILLUSTRATING?
REPEATING FOR EMPHASIS?
SUMMARISING?

4 **File your notes** for easy retrieval.

Figure 4.2

2 Concise summaries of the supporting detail.
3 Examples.
4 Simple diagrams (e.g. Figure 4.3).
5 Dates and numbers (if possible in a table, see Table 4.2).
6 Enough explanation to provide continuity.
7 Any new words.

8 All quotations, definitions, and summaries, dictated by the lecturer.

9 Details of any sources of information mentioned in the lecture.

Notes arranged in this way, preserving the order decided upon by the lecturer, and including all stages in any argument, are called linear or sequential notes. Such notes help you to recollect what was said in the lecture and any relevant discussion.

Remember that visual aids used in the lecture are not intended for your entertainment. They are part of the lecture and appropriate notes should be made. A good lecturer will not talk while writing or drawing and will give you time to study a completed diagram or visual aid before starting any explanation.

During the lecture, mark anything that you do not understand. For example, put a vertical line and a question mark in the margin. You can then ask a question at the end of the lecture or try to find the answer yourself before the next lecture.

Start each topic on a new sheet of notepaper and write on one side of each sheet only. You can then add sheets in the most appropriate places when you work on your notes later. Also, leave wide margins and plenty of space between lines of writing – for corrections and additions.

Creative pattern notes

An alternative, sometimes called the creative pattern method, is not sequential. The lecture title is written in the centre of a page, inside a circle, and then radiating lines are added to link this *central idea* to the topics covered in the lecture. Each topic is written as one or a few words (headings) and further lines radiate from each of these headings – pointing to supporting details each of which is noted as one key word or phrase. The result is a diagram (similar to Figure 5.3, page 74).

This method has the advantage that it makes the student listen to the lecture, concentrating not only on each main point but also on considering how it fits in to the picture as a whole. But these things can also be done by students who use the sequential method, who should also be recognizing topics and selecting appropriate sub-headings. Moreover, creative pattern notes have the following disadvantages.

1 The notes made, irrespective of the content of the lecture, are restricted to one page – unless a separate diagram is prepared for each topic covered in the lecture.
2 The notes must be restricted to key words or phrases. There is no space for whole sentences (e.g. definitions) or for complete bibliographic references, unless these are written on separate sheets, so that the student has to prepare creative pattern and sequential notes at the same time.
3 There is no space for corrections or additions in later study periods. For this reason, and also because the notes must be very rough, more work is needed after the lecture to produce another neater set of notes.
4 The student, looking at the notes later, cannot recapture the lecturer's train of thought. The plan of the lecture (topic outline) is lost in creating a non-sequential diagram.
5 A non-sequential record is unsuitable in some subjects (including mathematics and most engineering and science subjects) in which the logical development of an argument or proof must be recorded.

Table 4.2 Notes arranged in a table with annotations[a]

World region	Population[b] (millions)		Surface area (000s km²)
	1950	2000	
Africa	224	836	30 306
North America	166	308	21 517
Latin America	166	527	20 533
Asia	1403	3744	31 764
Europe	549	734	22 986
Oceania	13	31	8 537
World totals	2520	6169	135 641

Note
[a] To prevent mistakes in copying, notes of this kind are best provided by the lecturer as a hand-out.
[b] Based on data from UN (1997) *Statistical Yearbook*, New York, United Nations. The population estimates for 2000 calculated on the assumption that the annual rate of increase from 1995 to 2000 was the same as from 1990 to 1995.

Other kinds of notes

You will find it helpful to use different methods of note-making on different occasions – for different lectures and even for the parts of one lecture – depending upon your purpose and the way the material is presented for your consideration.

The notes taken in a lecture may be set out as a table (see Table 4.2) or as a diagram (see Figure 4.3), with annotations, to provide a convenient summary.

Also look at the notes made by other students during a lecture

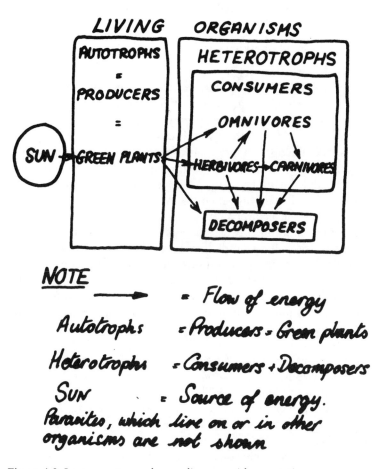

Figure 4.3 Lecture notes made as a diagram with annotations.

and compare them with your own. Are they about the same length as yours, and arranged in a similar way? Can you learn anything about note-making from them?

To give yourself practice in listening and selecting, and making notes, all at the same time, listen to a recorded talk. Make notes during the talk (see Figure 4.2); then play the recording again to check that you have noted the main points.

To make selection easier in class, do some preliminary reading. You can then concentrate on listening, picking out the main points (the things your lecturer considers important), understanding, noting, and appreciating the lecturer's approach.

Get into the habit of asking good questions

At the end of a lecture, if you have not already been given this information (a) ask for the lecturer's name, and (b) ask what the next lecture will be about, and (c) ask for a list of lecture titles, with dates, and suggestions for preliminary reading.

If there is time for questions or discussion during or at the end of a class, take the opportunity to ask for further explanation of any-thing that was not immediately clear. You are unlikely to be the only one who did not understand. Your questions will therefore help others and will encourage them to ask questions; and you should learn from all the lecturer's replies.

Questions not only help students to learn but also indicate interest in the subject, and this makes the lecturer's work more rewarding. Furthermore, questions should help the lecturer first to recognize things that students find difficult and then to give better lectures. More questions will come to mind during your further studies. Try to find the answers, before the next lecture (see Figure 4.4), in the ways discussed in Chapters 6 and 7. This will help you to learn.

Your success in filling gaps in your knowledge, by finding the answers to your own questions, will also help you to gain con-fidence as a student and will provide the basic understanding needed for further progress. You will also be encouraged, by your own efforts, to further effective study. However, there will be times when you do not find the information you need. You may also come across contradictions and then not know whom or what to believe. You should then ask good questions. You will

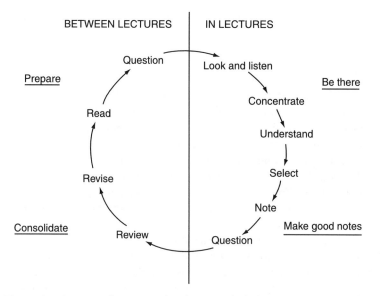

BETWEEN LECTURES | IN LECTURES

Figure 4.4 Aspects of active study: things to do before, during and after a lecture, tutorial or seminar.

find that some lecturers encourage questions and discussion during or at the end of each class. Others prefer to give individual help in tutorials.

Do not be afraid to go to see a lecturer to clear up any difficult point or to seek further guidance. If you choose an appropriate place and time most lecturers will welcome your interest in their subject. You should therefore get to know the special interests of all your lecturers so that when you have a problem you will know whom to consult. Go prepared, with your questions and notes or a textbook, so that you can pinpoint your difficulty and get help quickly.

AFTER THE LECTURE

A good lecturer will make your work easier, and more interesting, but you still have to do the work. The notes taken in a lecture provide a foundation upon which your knowledge can be built. They are not all that you need to know but they should provide a basis for further work. Thinking again about a lecture, *while it is fresh in your mind*, helps you to recall the lecture and is an aid to active study.

Review

As soon as possible after the lecture, preferably on the same evening, review your notes to make sure that you understand them now and that you will be able to understand them later. Check that they are an accurate record, including the date, a title, the most important points and enough supporting detail.

Do your best to master each subject (especially fundamentals) as you go along. Your early work is a basis for later work and so for progress on the course. Make a note of any questions that need to be answered or of any points that you do not fully understand. These are tasks for later study sessions.

Checking your notes and adding to them, where necessary, will help you to recall much of what was said in the lecture, will increase your understanding, and will help you to learn and to remember. However, do not get into the time-wasting habit of copying out notes neatly. If you are thinking during lectures and selecting carefully, you should be able to write legibly. If the lecture has been well organised (and if you made sequential notes, see page 51), you should have arranged your notes neatly, during the lecture, in a well organised sequence – similar to the topic outline prepared by the lecturer when deciding what to say. You need only brief notes that will be useful for both quick reference and revision. If the lecture has not been well planned, or if the lecturer has tried to say too much in the time available, you may not have been able to make good notes during the lecture: you will need to do more work on your notes while the lecture is fresh on your mind.

When you are satisfied with your notes on a lecture, mark the most important points, for emphasis, by numbering, underlining, or boxing (see Figure 4.2). Then look back at the previous lecture and at earlier lectures in the series, so that you can refresh your memory, review your progress, and see how the course is developing.

Study any hand-out supplied during the lecture. It may provide a summary of the main points made in the lecture (see Table 4.2), a diagram, or additions to what was said in the lecture. A lecturer who prepares a hand-out thinks it will be useful to you. Therefore, either read and then file it with your lecture notes, or incorporate material extracted from it in your lecture notes. If you throw even one hand-out away, without reading it, or if you file it in the wrong place, you may find that you are unable to answer a question set by this lecturer in one of your examinations.

Revise

Your review of a lecture, which should take perhaps twenty minutes, should be followed by about ten minutes of revision. From memory, list the most important points or basic essentials and write out any definitions. Then check to see that you have remembered correctly. This short time spent on revision will help to fix in your mind those things that you wish to remember. Before the next lecture, if you can, look at the sources of further information mentioned in this lecture.

GET THE MOST OUT OF GROUP WORK

Conversations and discussions provide opportunities to develop your communication skills. Contributing to discussions will help you to gain confidence in speaking about your subject and to develop your abilities to: (a) make your meaning clear, (b) argue logically and tactfully, (c) listen without interruption, (d) consider different points of view and different explanations, (e) observe the reactions of others to what is said, (f) ask searching questions, (g) disagree without causing offence, and (h) express opinions and state the evidence upon which they are based. In short, as you learn how to contribute effectively to discussions (see Figure 4.5), you learn about your subjects and develop your abilities to think and to communicate your thoughts.

Tutorials

In a tutorial a tutor meets a student (or a few students, see Figure 4.5) to discuss a previously arranged topic. Usually the tutor introduces the topic and encourages all present to participate. The tutor may also ask questions at appropriate points, to help the discussion along, and towards the end may indicate any omissions, sum up, and try to come to some conclusion.

Arrive at a tutorial prepared, having looked at the syllabus and at

SIT IN A CIRCLE SO THAT YOU CAN SEE EVERYONE

Figure 4.5 Be prepared to participate in discussions, but do not talk for too long.

your lecture notes on related topics. Perhaps you will have had time for some background reading. Be ready to participate in the discussion, and with a list of questions – so that you can try to clear up any difficulties or seek advice (for example, about background reading or sources of information on particular points).

The best preparation for a tutorial is probably to think about the topic to be discussed, as if you were preparing to write about it (see Table 4.3 and Chapter 5). You may then take to the tutorial: (a) a topic outline, (b) a list of questions, and (c) relevant lecture notes.

In the tutorial, take an active part in the discussion, but keep each of your contributions short and to the point. Ask for clarification (When?, Where?, How can that be?, Do you mean . . . ?). Ask other questions. Listen. Be responsive – by your facial expressions and by such comments as 'I understand' and 'That's interesting'. Be prepared to learn from all contributions. Make concise notes.

Seminars

More people are present at a seminar than at a tutorial, and one student may have been asked to introduce the topic that is to be discussed. All those present should have had the opportunity to

Table 4.3 Preparing for a discussion

Stages in preparation	Activities
Think	*List* relevant points. *Prepare* first draft of a topic outline.
Plan	*Note* difficulties encountered, gaps in your knowledge, and questions. Consult your own notes and references cited in lectures. Try to clear up difficulties, fill gaps, and answer questions or solve problems.
Write	*Revise* your topic outline. *Number* points you consider should be made in the discussion. *List* questions you would like to ask. *Listen* to the discussion. *Contribute*. State opinions and evidence. Explain. Ask questions. *Make notes*
Revise	After the discussion *review* your lecture notes on the subject and *revise* them if necessary.

consider the topic and, as for a tutorial, should arrive well prepared and ready to participate.

The first speaker should base a brief introduction (or presentation, see page 142), lasting about ten minutes, on a topic outline – and should draw attention to a few points that are topical or that for some other reason merit special attention at this seminar. All contributions to the discussion (comments, questions and answers) should be brief and to the point, so that anyone who wishes to contribute has the opportunity to do so. As with a tutorial, a seminar is an opportunity to learn. Take part in the discussion. Listen to other contributors. Make concise notes.

Such discussions should be interesting and stimulating. As you try to explain things, and listen to different interpretations of evidence, you think about your subjects and organise your thoughts. Then, after a tutorial or seminar, it is helpful to consider what you have learned. Amend your lecture notes so that all your notes on each topic are in one place (see pages 58 and 95). Going over things in your mind as you reconsider aspects of your work will help you to remember important points.

Self-help groups

Talking over a difficult point, after a class or after a period of private study, especially with someone who understands it better than you do, will help you with your work. And you will benefit from explaining things to others – just as teachers find that they learn more by teaching than they did, as students, from being taught.

Because conversation and discussion are aids to thinking, understanding, learning and remembering, you may find it helpful to join or organise a self-help group so that you can meet other students with similar interests and benefit regularly from group study – as in a tutorial but without a tutor.

Each meeting must have a definite purpose – agreed at the previous meeting, so that all can arrive well prepared. In some tutorials you may have the opportunity to discuss an assignment with a tutor, after it has been assessed. Similarly, in a self-help group you could discuss a tutor's comments written on your assignments and consider how you can benefit from any advice, or you could discuss some other previously agreed topic.

Discussing a topic with other students can help to fix the main points in your mind, as part of *revision*, and different ideas expressed may help you to see things in a new light. That is to say, taking part in a discussion is a stimulus to *thinking*. It can also add interest to your studies by providing a change from private study. It can provide *encouragement* by helping you to understand difficult points. As in teaching, explaining things to a friend will help you to make sure that you understand them yourself.

Participants in a discussion should approach it with an open mind. Having prepared, they should arrive at each meeting on time, with ideas they would like to share, prepared to consider different points of view, and to benefit from the experience. Then, a discussion works best if everyone contributes.

Arrive prepared to speak but do not attempt to say all that you might like to say at once. *Speak clearly and concisely* each time you make a point. You will be surprised to find how much can be said in one minute; and two minutes with the same person talking would begin to sound more like a lecture than a contribution to a discussion. *Listen carefully*, therefore, and *time your remarks* so that you speak only when you have something immediately relevant to say. For example, in discussing a problem you might speak early, add ideas from time to time, argue for or against particular approaches, and suggest a possible solution.

It helps when working in a group, as in a committee, if someone agrees to lead the discussion (perhaps a different person for each meeting so that each student gains experience of this role). The leader can: (a) remind participants of the purpose of the meeting (the topic or problem to be discussed), (b) encourage contributions from all those present, (c) discourage individuals who talk too often or for too long, (d) ensure that all contributions are relevant, and (e) towards the end of the meeting try to summarise the main points raised, state any conclusion agreed or decision made – including the choice of topic for discussion at the next self-help group meeting.

Members of a group that meets regularly may come to think of themselves as a team and benefit from *team-work* in many ways that they could not have foreseen, and which will differ from group to group. They may agree to work together in the first place because of their course of study, but by getting to know one another better and sharing personal problems, as well as study problems, they may become life-long friends.

Self-help group meetings can be particularly useful for those studying part-time or mainly by taking correspondence courses, or using other distance learning materials, who otherwise would have little contact with people who shared their interests. For such people, especially, e-mail can provide another convenient means of contact with a tutor; and computer conferencing can provide a notice board on which students leave messages and receive comments and advice – from other students or from their tutor.

WRITING PAPER AND STORAGE MATERIALS

The notes you make in lectures, tutorials, seminars, and other organised classes, and when discussing things with a tutor or other students, provide a foundation for all your other work as a student. As you review and revise your work after classes, you revise your notes. You add to them, revise them and condense them as you obtain information from other sources and increase your under-standing of your work. So it is very important to consider, early in your studies, not only how you can improve your note-making skills but also what writing materials and storage materials you should use. However, you are advised not to buy them before your course begins because you may be given definite instructions, for example, about the writing materials to be used for assessed course work. It is also best to seek the advice of your course leader, class lecturer or personal tutor before purchasing any special equipment that may be needed for your course (for example, a calculator and drawing instruments).

Writing paper

Wide-lined A4 paper (210 × 297 mm) with a 25 mm margin is provided in most examinations, and it is a good idea to use this kind of paper for all your written work, unless you are instructed to do otherwise. Narrow-lined paper is a false economy – because, for written work, there is no space between the lines for minor additions or for a marker's comments and corrections. The cost of paper is small, compared with the cost of your education, and it is worth giving yourself space in which to work.

It is probably best to carry enough loose-leaf paper for one day's notes (in an envelope or folder), and to write on one side of each page only, so that the notes made during the day can be transferred to appropriate files, kept at home, each evening. This reduces the chances of losing all your notes on a subject. Also, pages can be inserted, rearranged or removed, easily, whenever necessary. Bound notebooks, which are useful to a pupil at school for notes dictated by a teacher, are not recommended for students who are making their own notes – except in laboratory and field work when the use of a bound notebook helps to ensure that, as in a diary, each day's work is dated and entries are in chronological order.

Storing your notes

Your notes are for use, not for permanent storage. They are the basis for active study: not a graveyard in which ideas can rest in peace. They should be readily available for consultation, for regular use in revision, and for the addition of ideas, information and examples.

If you use loose-leaf paper, as recommended, your notes on each subject may be stored at home. Keep them either in A4 envelopes that will accept the paper without folding, or in clearly labelled manilla folders. Store the envelopes in box files or, as a cheap alternative, in large cereal packets from which one side or one end has been removed. If you prefer to use folders, light-weight manilla folders are probably best. Ring-binders are bulky even when empty and they do not hold the paper firmly.

Index cards (or postcards) are useful. Use a separate card for a complete bibliographic record (see page 92) of each source of information that you have found useful, so that you can consult the same source again if necessary. You may also find index cards useful when you prepare your own concise revision aids. Small index cards (125 × 75 mm) are large enough for most purposes and they can be stored in a cardboard shoe box.

There is no need, as a student, for you to spend money on expensive hard-backed folders, box files, or filing drawers. Your money is better spent on writing paper and necessary reference books.

5

Think and learn

A philatelist may remember every stamp in a large collection, and a card player the order in which all cards were played in a game. Similarly, you can remember interesting things. To master a new subject you need only to start at the beginning, have a desire to learn, take an active interest, and use effective study techniques.

ORGANISE AND SELECT

This is the sequence in effective study:

1 Select things to record as you observe, listen, or read.
2 Review your notes to make sure that you do understand them and that they are well organised.
3 Recognise the fundamentals and select other important points that you wish to remember.
4 Mark these things for emphasis – so that they stand out from the supporting detail when you . . .
5 Revise and try to remember.

There is no point in trying to remember things that you do not understand; and you would have great difficulty if you tried to learn pages of notes parrot-fashion. Also, such rote learning is usually a waste of time because most questions set in course work and examinations call for understanding as well as knowledge.

In marking it is easy to distinguish passages that a student has copied from a textbook, or remembered from lecture notes, without understanding. Few marks can be given for the display of knowledge that you have not made your own (see also plagiarism, page 112); and examination *howlers* or *boners* are blunders that occur when students try to write about half-remembered things that they do not understand.

HOW TO REMEMBER

1 Pay attention when new topics are introduced in class, or as you are reading. *First impressions make a great impact.* A good lecturer or author can help you to learn by making your first experience of each topic accurate, understandable, and interesting. Similarly, you can help yourself by concentrating and getting things right the first time.

2 Shortly after learning something, you may remember most of it. But as time goes by you may forget more and more. Therefore, revise each topic soon after you learn it (see Table 5.1) and then *keep each aspect of your work fresh in your mind.*

3 Learning is aided by concentrating on *one task at a time.* This is why half an hour of active study is better than a longer period of half-hearted or poorly directed effort.

4 *Learning and remembering are aided by association.* It helps you to remember if each new thought can be linked to things you already know, or if things you wish to learn can be arranged in a pattern or diagram.

5 *Learning is aided by the use of different senses*: by seeing, hearing and writing in lectures; and by seeing and touching in practical work. Learning is helped if you can confirm or find things out for yourself.

6 *Learning is easiest if things give you pleasure.* Pleasure may come from listening to an enthusiastic teacher, from reading a good book, from increased knowledge and understanding, and from good marks awarded or praise received.

7 *Learning and remembering are aided by repetition.* Some students find their work easy but have difficulty in remembering. Others have initial difficulties but then retain the knowledge. This is probably because, in trying to understand, they have had to think about the work again and again.

Repetition helps to fix things in your mind. You may remember more, therefore, if you read something twice quickly in preference to once slowly (see also page 94). Similarly, whatever you wish to learn and remember, you will probably find it most effective to devote several short study periods to the task rather than a single long one. In the later periods you add to what you have already absorbed; this method of learning things for the first time (little by little) incorporates the beneficial effects of revision. This is another reason for breaking longer study sessions into shorter periods of active study (see page 39).

Revise regularly

Revision should be a regular part of active study. At the start of every study period it is a good idea to spend two minutes thinking about how the work fits into your previous studies. Also, end every study period with a few minutes devoted to a review and to revision; consider what you have achieved or learned and, if appropriate, list the main points as a concise summary.

On the following week-end, or as soon as possible after learning something for the first time, work on your notes again. Check again that you understand. If you have not already done so, mark important points (see page 58) and add examples as an aid to remembering. Make sure that the things you wish to remember are in an order that suits your purpose.

What you already know provides an organised basis for further work. You must, therefore, master your subject step by step. Without a grasp of the fundamentals you will have no basis for understanding the more advanced work – just as if you miss one lecture you may not understand the next (see Figure 4.1, page 47).

Study each topic again and again: by preliminary reading; by attending lectures and other organised classes; by checking and reviewing your notes; by revising on the following week-end; when reviewing your later lectures in the same series; each time you use your knowledge of the subject (for example in preparing topic outlines and summaries); in each vacation; and before examinations (see Table 5.1).

Working on your notes helps you to recall what was said in a lecture (or what you have read or observed). You see the most important points emphasised. You see diagrams. You review your

Table 5.1 Repetition as part of active study

	Activity	Time	Spacing your revision
1	Preliminary reading	Day before class	—12 hours
2	Listen		
3	Make notes	In class	
4	Discuss		—6 hours
5	Check notes	Same evening	
			—4 days
6	Review and revise	Next weekend	
7	Revise	When you review next lecture	—4 days
			—6 weeks
8	Review	Each time you use your knowledge	—? ?
9	Revise	Next vacation	—12 weeks
		Next vacation	
			—6 weeks
10	Revise	Before examination	

progress and see each topic as part of a whole. You recognise your weaknesses and can work on them. You identify key concepts and make connections between topics and subjects. You understand more and more. Regular revision, therefore, is an essential part of active study. Good students attend to each subject regularly and not just in a last desperate attempt to learn things for the first time in the weeks before an examination.

Learn some things by heart

People of any age can fix things in their minds by repeating them aloud once a day for about a week. This is the way to learn new words, spelling, short quotations, poems, definitions, laws, rules, important dates, multiplication tables, formulae, symbols, and similar fundamentals of your subject. See also revision notes, page 167.

If things you must remember can be said as a rhyme, or with a certain rhythm, it is easy to say them again and again until they cannot be forgotten. For example, in spelling:

When the sound is ee
Remember
i before e
except after c.

And in different languages there are rhymes to help children
remember how many days there are in each month.

Thirty days hath September,
April, June and November.
All the rest have thirty-one,
Except February with twenty-eight.
And, once in four,
February shall have one day more.

Some people find it helpful to remember a memory cue or mne-
monic. For example, the initial letters of the sentence 'Richard of
York Gave Battle in Vain' should help you to recall the order of
colours in a spectrum: Red, Orange, Yellow, Green, Blue, Indigo,
and Violet. However, learning too many mnemonics could lead to
confusion – making it harder to remember instead of easier.

USE YOUR KNOWLEDGE

When you learn a language, it is easiest to remember new words if
you use them regularly in appropriate contexts. Similarly, whatever
you study, try to use all your knowledge of each subject at every
appropriate opportunity (see Figure 5.4, page 75).

1 Consider any practical applications of each aspect of your work.
2 When you have a question to answer in course work or in examinations, consider all aspects of your work (see page 72), so that
   you can recall relevant material and select from all that you know.
3 Set yourself questions as a test (see page 71) so that you can use
   your newly acquired knowledge, draw upon different aspects of
   your work as an aid to revision, and practise writing a good
   answer in the time that would be available in an examination.
4 Construct flow charts and other diagrams (like Figure 4.3, page
   55) that will help you to organise your thoughts, contribute to
   your understanding, and be useful as revision aids. Many things
   can be represented diagramatically and you may find it easier to
   visualise diagrams than to remember words alone.

5 Write out things that you must remember, from memory, and then check that they are correct. Using your knowledge in this way should be a regular part of your revision.

6 When you think you understand something, try to explain it simply to a friend (see Figure 5.1). Alternatively, try to explain it to yourself, in writing, and then check your own work. Either way, you will have to arrange your thoughts and confirm that you do understand. Then you can make a note of any new insights – or of the need for further work.

Plan answers to questions

TRY TO EXPLAIN SOMETHING
SIMPLY TO A FRIEND

Figure 5.1 Before you can explain anything you must understand it yourself.

Thinking about questions and planning answers, as well as being a preparation for writing (see page 120), is a method of active study (see Figure 8.3, page 118) that helps you: (a) to distinguish main points from supporting detail; (b) to select the most appropriate examples; (c) to develop an ability to select only relevant material and, therefore, to reject anything that is irrelevant; (d) to organize relevant information and ideas; and (e) to recognise gaps in your knowledge.

Think. When you are sure what the question means (see page 136), make a note of any terms in the question. In your answer you must make clear that you understand their meaning, either by defining them or by using them correctly in appropriate contexts.

Consider carefully what is needed for a complete answer to the question asked. Write words and phrases, spread over a whole page (or screen), as you think about the main parts of your answer (see Figure 5.2). These will serve as subheadings, below which you can add further notes as you think of relevant information, examples and ideas that might be included in each part.

Some people prefer to record their thoughts in a diagram (see Figure 5.3). You will find which way suits you best: in both you can distinguish main points from supporting detail or examples, and arrows can be used to indicate possible connections – which may help you to decide upon an effective order for your paragraphs.

As you record your first thoughts on any subject, you can help yourself to recall relevant topics by asking yourself the six questions from Rudyard Kipling's poem *The Serving Men*. Their names are: What? Why? When? How? Where? and Who? Your answers to these one word questions can never be just yes or no (see Figure 3.2, page 36). Usually, by recording your replies to these questions, you will find that you know much more about many subjects than you had at first realised.

Another way in which you can stimulate your thoughts is to consider different aspects of your subject, or to wonder how the question would be tackled by specialists in different branches of your subject – or by people with differing points of view. Such thoughts may help you to bring together topics that are relevant to your answer, but which did not immediately come to mind when you first read the question.

Plan. Work on your preliminary notes, prepared as you thought about the question. Add numbers (as in Figures 5.2 and 5.3) as you decide on the order of paragraphs. How is your answer to be introduced? What is to be the topic for each paragraph? How can your answer be drawn to a satisfactory conclusion?

After even a few minutes of thought and reflection you may have decided on the main parts of your answer and made a note of many points that could be included in each part. Indeed, because planning is itself a stimulus to thinking, you must always think and plan before you write.

In an examination you may be able to spare only a few minutes for preliminary thoughts and for planning your answer. In course

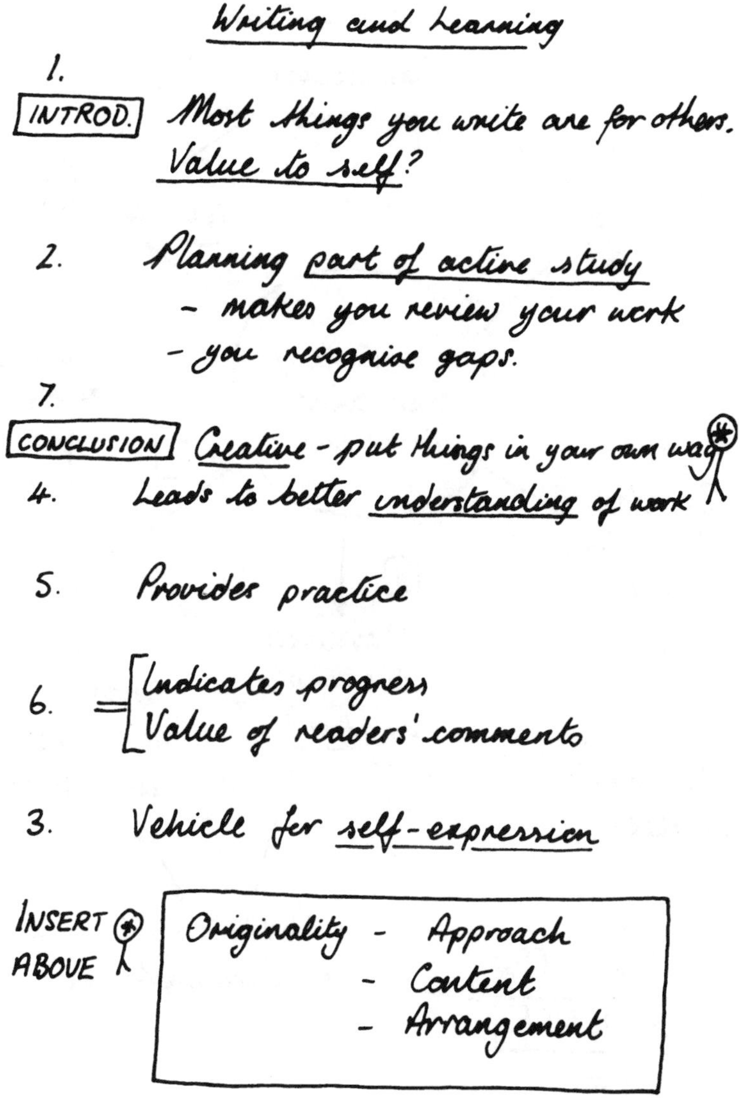

Writing and Learning

1.
[INTROD.] Most things you write are for others.
Value to self?

2. Planning part of active study
   - makes you review your work
   - you recognise gaps.

7.
[CONCLUSION] Creative - put things in your own way ✱

4. Leads to better understanding of work

5. Provides practice

6. ⎡ Indicates progress
    ⎣ Value of readers' comments

3. Vehicle for self-expression

INSERT ✱
ABOVE ↖ ⎡ Originality - Approach
          - Content
          - Arrangement ⎤

Figure 5.2 First thoughts for a composition on the importance of writing in study, with relevant points listed as they came to mind – then numbered after further thought to indicate the order of paragraphs in a topic outline or plan.

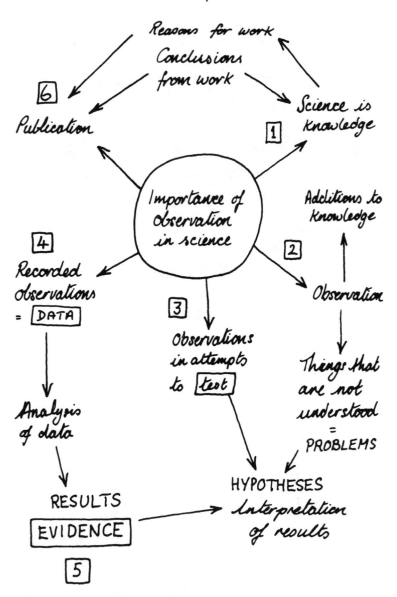

Figure 5.3 First thoughts for a composition on the importance of observation in science, recorded as creative pattern notes – then with numbers added after further thought – to indicate the order of paragraphs in a topic outline or plan.

work you have more time but your first step should still be to think about the question and make concise notes of things that should be in your answer. Always do this before looking at your lecture notes or at other sources of information, so that you can: *ensure a fresh approach*; consider which aspects of your work may be relevant; test your memory and understanding; and recognise where further information is needed. This is also good practice for examinations in which you must rely on what you know.

Having prepared a plan, look at your lecture notes or at other sources of information (see Chapters 6 and 7) so that you can fill any gaps, learn more about your subject, and then give a more complete answer to the question asked.

EXERCISE YOUR MIND

The techniques for thinking, understanding and remembering, recommended in this chapter involve the regular revision of all subjects, and of all parts of each subject. Regular revision, learning by heart, and using your knowledge in conversation and writing, all make you think about your work repeatedly (see Figure 5.4). This helps you to understand, to see connections, and to remember.

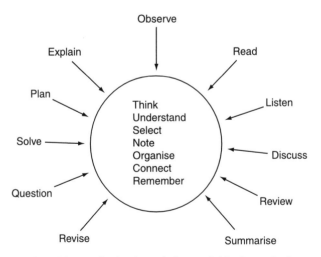

Figure 5.4 Acquiring and using knowledge: activities in study that contribute to learning.

We all forget things in which we are not interested – because we rarely think about them. Good students, however, attend to each subject regularly (see page 68). This does not mean that they have to do more work than other students. On the contrary, they avoid last minute cramming and make their work easier: (a) by spreading the load, (b) because each time they revise it is easier to refresh the memory than the time before, and (c) because each time they revise they see connections between recent work and their earlier studies.

6

Observe and learn

Thinking and planning enable you to set down what you know and to recognize gaps in your knowledge. Your purpose in study should then be to fill these gaps, so that you can understand each subject better and give more complete answers to questions.

In all subjects which bear upon everyday experience there are many things that you can find out for yourself. In many ways this is the best way to learn: you are likely to remember things that you have seen and noted (but see Figure 6.1). In practical work in a laboratory, studio or workshop, therefore, it is not enough to follow instructions. You must think about your work; use your knowledge; confirm things that you have been told or read; use these opportunities to learn. For the same reasons, approach field work, organised visits, and opportunities to travel, with enthusiasm. By observation you can broaden and extend your experience. Also, in all these activities a supervisor will be present to answer your questions, discuss any problems, and help in other ways.

DIFFICULTIES IN THE WAY OF ACCURATE OBSERVATION

You may regard things you have seen as facts, but observation is not easy. The following are some reasons why observers make incomplete and inaccurate observations.

YOU ARE LIKELY TO REMEMBER THINGS YOU HAVE SEEN FOR YOURSELF

Figure 6.1 A student, like anyone else, has a limited ability to maintain attention and make complete and accurate observations.

(a) Inadequate preparation

Satisfactory practical work depends upon adequate preparation.

Self. You must know what you are doing and why it is worthwhile. You should be in the right state of mind. This is why practical exercises usually follow lectures on the subject or, in project work, they follow background reading, a literature survey, or preliminary observations.

Equipment. Many instruments are used as aids to observation. They extend your ability to observe (for example telescopes and oscilloscopes) or to make precise measurements (for example rulers and thermometers), but you must know how to use any equipment and how to check that it is working properly.

Materials. In science subjects all glassware, for example, must be clean, and all chemicals must be pure.

Methods. The procedure to be followed must be clearly stated. This is why a practical schedule is usually provided for each class.

Such preparations are necessary so that a clear statement can be made of the conditions under which observations were made; so that the observations recorded are accurate (i.e. can be regarded as data); and so that, if necessary, similar observations can be made again under similar conditions.

(b) Lack of concentration throughout an observation

A break in attention may be due to distraction, to the need to look away to use an instrument or make a note, or to fatigue. In *Shane*, Jack Schaefer (1954) describes the habitual alertness of a man whose life depends on careful and accurate observation – his eyes endlessly searching, 'checking off every item in view, missing nothing'. A sustained effort is needed if a description is to be accurate and complete. This is why preparing an accurate drawing or diagram, which makes you look carefully, is an aid to complete and accurate description: you must look at each part of an object or scene separately to see the details as well as the whole.

(c) Abstraction

In *Jeremy*, Hugh Walpole (1919) writes of a man – seen every day – who was to Jeremy 'shrouded by an invisibility of tradition'. In everyday life you ignore many things. Life would be unbearable without such abstraction, but the result is that you may disregard things which later assume some importance. In making observations, be aware of this difficulty that stands in the way of complete and accurate observation.

(d) Inexperience

When you see something for the first time you are like an explorer venturing into the unknown. The difficulty of seeing all when there is much to see, and you do not know what to look for is well illustrated by the inside of a gypsy's caravan as imagined by a child in *Thrush Green* (Miss Read, 1959), 'with so many things to see that it would be hard to distinguish separate objects'.

(e) Experience

Although preparation is necessary, reading before you investigate may direct your mind along well worn tracks and away from a fresh approach to a problem. Knowing what to expect may also be a barrier to complete and accurate observation.

> It is that which we do know which is the greatest hindrance to our learning, not that which we do not know.
>
> Claude Bernard (1813–1878)

Taking things for granted. Many things happen with such regularity that you may come to accept that they always happen. There may then be occasions when you are prepared to believe that something has happened when it has not.

Seeing only the expected. When you observe an event, with many things happening together, you may see only some of these things – even if you observe the same sequence many times (as in a film). You may have had the experience, if you have seen a film more than once, of seeing more in your second and third observations of the same events. Perhaps certain things captured your attention: these may have been the things that you expected to see. Because it is sometimes difficult to see more than expected, and so add to observations, it may be difficult to make original observations.

For example, H. R. Hanson (1963) in *The Concept of the Positron* tells how for two years after the existence of positrons had been predicted, their tracks in cloud chamber photographs of cosmic rays were ignored or interpreted as artefacts.

Seeing only the unexpected. Sometimes you may fail to see familiar things, that are expected, because your attention has been captured by something that does not usually happen, or that has gone unnoticed previously. Your record of the observation may then be incomplete – because only the unexpected event can be adequately recorded.

Stuck in a groove. By making observations in the same way, day after day, you may record useful data. But what you see will be limited by the method used. Because of this fixed routine, you may be less likely to break new ground than would be someone coming new to the project who looked at things in a new way.

Previous experience. In 1928 Alexander Fleming was interested in the bactericidal properties of natural secretions, such as tears. His later observation that no bacteria were growing in the part of a culture medium contaminated by the fungus *Penicillium*, was the first step that lead to the discovery and isolation of the antibiotic penicillin. Because the contamination of the culture was not planned, the observation of the effect of the contaminant was made possible by an accident, yet Fleming's mind was prepared by his previous experience: he considered the possible importance of an observation that another scientist might have ignored.

In science most discoveries are made by accident in experiments designed for other purposes – but they are made by scientists who spend time at their workbench and are, therefore, in a position to make observations and to take advantage of their luck.

Previous experience may also make observation more rather than less difficult. For example, we believe things to be true when we have seen them ourselves – but it is difficult to guard against optical illusions (Figure 6.2). This is why scientists, to achieve precision, make careful measurements.

Preconceived ideas. Our ability to see things, or to believe what we see, is restricted by our preconceived ideas. People are reluctant to accept new ideas, especially if these conflict with their beliefs.

For example, in 1514, Nicholas Copernicus made observations which indicated that Earth orbited the sun. At first he was reluctant to publish his findings because religious leaders taught that the world had been created at the centre of the heavens: they insisted that the world was flat, and that the sun moved around Earth. In 1616 a congregation of political and religious leaders condemned his work (which had eventually been published in 1543) and placed it on a list of prohibited books.

We also find it difficult to make or to accept observations that are outside our previous experience. It is easy to understand why there was a general mistrust of travellers' tales, before the use of photography and television allowed many people to see things for themselves.

Even with these aids to accurate reporting we may still detect bias in accounts of a recent event – reported, but probably not observed, by two journalists with opposing political views. If, therefore, it is not possible to know what happened yesterday in London or New York, at an event that was widely reported, it is even more difficult to find out what happened in the past. Indeed, there are countries

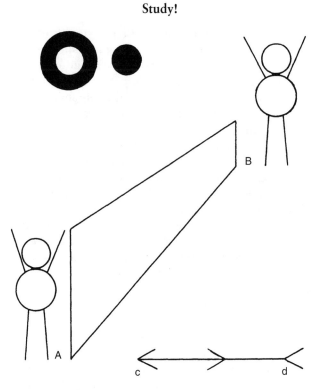

Figure 6.2 Can you believe what you see? Would the black disc fit into the black ring? Who is the taller, A or B? Where is the mid-point on the horizontal line cd?

where it is the duty of historians to abolish the past. Such a role is nothing new for historians. In most societies, in most eras, they have received official countenance only on condition that they subscribed to and reinforced the reigning dogmas (see Howard, M., 1981, *The Lessons of History*).

MAKE NOTES AS YOU OBSERVE

Before making observations, as part of an investigation, make adequate preparations, then concentrate throughout the observation and be aware of the kinds of difficulties that stand in the way of complete and accurate observation and recording data.

In preparing for an enquiry or investigation most observers plan to record certain kinds of data, perhaps at regular intervals, in a table or data sheet. The first column of many data sheets (the stubb) has the heading *Date* or *Time*, and each of the other columns has a heading to indicate what is to be observed or measured each time entries are made, and the units of measurement.

The data sheet: (a) is an aid to planning the procedure – as you decide what observations should be recorded. Then during the enquiry or investigation the data sheet: (b) serves as a reminder of when observations are to be made and of what is to be recorded; (c) facilitates the preparation of records as observations are made; and, therefore, (d) helps to ensure that there is a concise, complete and accurate record. And afterwards: (e) the orderly arrangement of the data facilitates their interpretation and analysis.

Most data sheets include a column for comments so that, for example, any unexpected observations can be recorded and any necessary explanations. If your data sheet is to be included in a report (for example for assessment), a carbon copy should be kept (for safe-keeping) as your observations are recorded. Data recorded during observations should not be rewritten, because mistakes may be made in copying.

RESULTS OF THE ANALYSIS OF DATA

Observations, once recorded, are called data. The word *data* refers to facts of any kind: things known to be true. It is incorrect, therefore, to refer to real data or raw data.

Data recorded, in order as observations are made, may not be easy to interpret. The next step in an investigation, therefore, is usually their analysis. With numerical data this analysis may involve the use of statistical methods. However, calculations may not be needed. It may be sufficient to present the data in a diagram.

If data can be interpreted without analysis we may say that the result of the investigation is obvious. If statistical analysis is necessary, the result of this analysis is called a *result*. It is easy, therefore, to distinguish between data and results, although some people use these words incorrectly – as if they were synonyms.

Note particularly that no amount of care in the rearrangement or statistical analysis of data can compensate for inadequate preparation, for lack of care in observation, or for errors in measuring or recording. Careful observation and precise measurement come first, accompanied by the preparation of accurate records. Statistical analysis may then be desirable, but the results should be interpreted with care. For example, always remember the following points.

1 The result should not be expressed in more places of decimals than are present in the least accurately known component of the calculation; otherwise your result will appear to be more accurate than is possible with the method of measurement used in obtaining the data.
2 If things are improbable this does not mean that they never happen, and they may happen in your investigation.
3 If two things are correlated this does not mean that one is necessarily the cause of the other.
4 If a curved or straight line can be drawn through the data points on a graph, this does not mean that they should be so connected. To do so is to infer and imply that intermediate points (had you recorded them) would have been on this line.

PREPARING A REPORT ON AN INVESTIGATION

If you are expected to write an account of an enquiry or investigation, or of any practical exercise, you should be given sufficient information and advice about what is expected in your particular course.

In practical classes stay until the end. Make full use of these opportunities to learn by handling materials, practising techniques, making observations, and asking questions. Try to complete practical exercises and prepare neat records (date, title, materials, methods and observations) in class, so that you need spend little more time on them. The practice of re-writing class notes neatly is unacceptable because, almost inevitably, mistakes are made in copying.

Instead of spending time on *writing up* practical work, more time should be devoted to thinking about the purpose of the exercise (which should be stated clearly in your *Introduction*) and considering what can be learned from it (in your *Discussion* and *Conclusions*).

7

Read and learn

There are many things that you could not find out for yourself, by observation, even in a lifetime. You must therefore make time for reading books and other publications as sources of information and ideas. Reading is a key to knowledge, and a good library a university open to everyone. Indeed, undergraduate students attend lectures and other organised classes but are still said to be *reading* for a degree.

So many books and journals are published every year that it is impossible for any library to buy them all. However, this does not mean that every year there is more for students to learn. On the contrary, observing things that are not understood may be followed by the formulation of hypotheses. Further observations may provide evidence that helps people to reject some hypotheses, so that more knowledge means that there may be less for students to learn. Also, after many observations have been made, links are seen between previously isolated facts and things seem to fall into place. Recognizing a pattern makes things easier to understand.

Some Greek philosophers attempted to record all knowledge. No one could think of doing this today: so much is known. As a result people specialise; it is said that we learn more and more about less and less. In most degree courses the student starts by studying a variety of subjects but specialises, in later years, in aspects of one subject. Syllabuses, therefore, do not cover the whole of any subject.

Only selected aspects are introduced in lectures, seminars, tutorials, and other organised classes.

DECIDE WHAT TO READ

In most subjects you will not be expected to read the whole of every article or book mentioned in lectures or included in the reading lists provided at the start of a course. Other students will tell you which books they found interesting and useful, but remember that their needs and their evaluation may differ from yours. You need to develop the ability to test and assess any composition for yourself – carefully but *in no more time than is necessary*.

Preliminary survey

To test a book, undertake a quick survey or trial reading, but *read no further than you consider necessary*. Certain questions will be in your mind:

> What do I want to know?
> Is this book likely to be useful to me?
> If it is, should I read the whole book, read selected chapters, refer to certain pages, or just note the complete bibliographic details (see page 92) for future reference?

Look not only at the title but also to see if there is a subtitle: this is printed on the title page, immediately below the title, but not necessarily on the cover. The title and subtitle, together, should give a good indication of what the book is about.

Is this publication sufficiently up-to-date for your present needs? Glance at the date on the reverse of the title page, to see when the book was published and how recently it was revised, so that you will know how up-to-date the information given in the book could be. Note that a book is normally revised for a new edition but not for a reprint.

Is it at the right level for you at this stage in your course? Read the preface which should indicate the author's purpose and intentions. This may tell you that the book is an introduction to the subject, or that it is for advanced students, or that it is a textbook for a particular course.

What is its scope? Scan the table of contents. This also indicates the author's approach, not only by the selection of material for inclusion but also by the order of chapters. From the sequence of topics and the scope of the book, you can appreciate the author's purpose. You can see if the book as a whole is likely to provide a balanced treatment of the subject or is concerned mainly with selected aspects.

Does it contain the information you require? Use the contents page or the index so that you can look up something you are already familiar with, to see how the topic is treated in this book. Look up topics in which you are currently interested and read the relevant paragraphs.

How do these parts fit into the composition as a whole? Skim through the book. Read a paragraph or two in each chapter and the headings, and the chapter summaries if there are any. Look at the diagrams and tables. Read especially the last few pages.

Is this book likely to be useful to you? Look at other books before deciding which are likely to be of most use to you. This is particularly important when buying a textbook for your course. However, when selecting books in a library, always consider if each book is relevant to your immediate needs. You may need a general introduction to the subject or a book on a particular aspect. Perhaps you need both so that you can read one chapter from one book and selected pages from the other. If a book looks useful, always consider how you should use it.

DECIDE HOW TO READ

If you read and re-read in an attempt to fix things in your mind, your reading is likely to become more and more passive. In re-reading you recognise what you have seen before, rather than learning, and your mind may even be on other things.

As a student *your reading must be active*. In reading, as in other aspects of study, take control. *Decide* whether to read, which parts to read, and how to read. Just as in driving a car you can brake by going into a lower gear, so in reading you can spend more time on a passage than is worthwhile by employing a reading technique that is not suited to your immediate purpose.

There is more than one way to read a book: you do not have to start on page one and read through to the end. Read according to *your purpose*. Read some books to enjoy the language and the story. Use others as sources of information and ideas. Usually, as a student, you will be: surveying the contents pages of textbooks to discover the scope of the subject, to identify its parts, and to see the approaches of different authors; or reading before classes so that you can benefit more from class work than would otherwise be possible; or looking for information on specific points; or undertaking background reading to confirm and extend your knowledge.

Scanning

Scan the contents pages or index, so that you can go directly to relevant pages of a book, encyclopaedia or journal. If you cannot find a word in the index, try a synonym. Then, if necessary, look at the contents pages to see which chapter or section is most likely to contain the information you require. Scan these pages – not reading them but *looking for particular words* – so that you find relevant sentences quickly. Read these carefully.

Skim reading

When you find a book that contains the information you require, let your eyes skim the pages. You do not need to read every word. Notice the signposts provided by the author: chapter headings, sub-headings, words in **bold print** or *italics*, and numbered lists. Look at the tables and diagrams. Read the first paragraph of each chapter, and perhaps the first sentence of each paragraph – which will probably indicate what the chapter or paragraph is about. Read the chapter summaries. In this skim reading you will ignore some paragraphs and even some chapters because they seem irrelevant to your present needs. In this way you will find relevant parts quickly, select relevant material that is new to you, and see how this fits into an organised whole. It will help you, to get a quick overview, if you do not wish to spend long on reading a composition, to *read for the main idea* instead of reading every word.

Rapid reading

When children learn to read, the letters are unfamiliar. They may say each letter aloud before pronouncing the word as a whole. As the words become familiar they read word by word, without difficulty, but may still read aloud. Many adults read slowly because they have not got beyond this word by word stage. The eyes focus on each word and, perhaps, each word is mouthed even though it is not spoken. Saying or mouthing words prevents faster reading – because most people can learn to read much faster than they can speak.

Slow reading is unlikely to be a handicap in studying most subjects, but if you have to do a lot of reading you may wish to increase your reading speed. Check that you do not mouth the words, or stare at each word as you come to it. If necessary, make an effort to improve your vocabulary by reading good prose and looking up unfamiliar words in a dictionary, so that you are not held up by words that you do not understand.

To increase your reading speed, even if you already read quite quickly, make your eyes move forward, allowing them to stop only four, three or two times, as you learn to move them faster along each line. You will soon find that you are reading two or three words at a time. Do not allow your eyes, as they move forward, to glance back at words gone by. Practice rapid reading regularly – at first with light reading matter.

Reading faster does not mean reading non-stop. *Adjust your method of reading and your reading speed according to your purpose* (see Table 7.1). When necessary, pause for thought, consider what you have read in relation to your previous knowledge, and make notes so that your reading is active. Reading faster will not mean that you assimilate less. On the contrary, you are likely to concentrate more easily, grasp the author's meaning sooner, understand better, and remember more.

Reading critically

Whatever you read, be it a whole book or one chapter, or a short article, always begin with a preliminary survey. Note the author's approach, purpose, and style of writing. *Consider your purpose.* Why are you spending time on this activity?

Table 7.1 Reading to some purpose: adjust your method of reading and your reading speed according to your purpose

Technique	Purpose
Trial reading	Quick survey so that you can decide if, when and how the composition may be of use to you.
Scanning	Rapid search for particular words, for example in the index or on text pages.
Skimming	Quick overview of a composition to find parts that are of immediate interest, and to see how these fit in as part of the composition.
Rapid reading	Light reading for pleasure, and as part of active study.
Critical reading	Slower reading, to weigh and consider, to assess, and perhaps to make notes.

Do you have to answer a question that calls for description, criticism, evaluation etc. (see page 136)? If you are looking for information (details relating to topics) you will scan to find the relevant page or pages quickly. If you are looking for ideas (additional topics) you may skim read to find them quickly. In either case, having selected the parts that are worth active study, you will understand, learn and remember more if you read them twice. First read quickly, as in reading a novel, and then undertake a more critical reading.

> Concentrate.
> Think carefully to make sure that you understand.
> Look back, if necessary, to check the stages in an argument.
> Be prepared to consider opinions that differ from your own.
> Weigh the evidence and look for contradictions.
> Read with an enquiring and critical mind.

If the author asks a question, consider your answer before you read on. Ask yourself questions. Why is this relevant? What does this mean? Is the evidence convincing? Is the composition biased? What have I learned? Such questions will help you to concentrate and to think critically. For example, see *Criticise the work of other writers*, page 121.

Your reactions as you read should be influenced by your previous experience, just as authors in writing build on their experiences. You should not believe every word that you read. Try to distinguish evidence from opinion. Remember that even when there is a basis of fact in every paragraph, the interpretation may be wrong.

Many things are written to convince or to persuade: they are not impartial. You must weigh the evidence presented and try to make up your own mind. Read critically and consider how the information and ideas presented contribute to your understanding and fit in with your knowledge gained from other sources. You may conclude, having considered different sides of an argument, that the truth is not known.

At school you may have thought that every word in your textbooks was to be believed and remembered. However, the more you read books by specialists the more you will find that there are many points on which they disagree. This is why it is best to use more than one textbook on each aspect of your course and to consult other sources of information and ideas. As a student you should not be trying to learn what you have been told or what you have read: by thinking and questioning you should be aiming at a better understanding, as you master your subject.

MAKE NOTES AS YOU READ

Many of the books you consult are not your own. You should not mark them in any way. Furthermore, you are advised not to mark even your own textbooks. When you first read a book you will be learning about the subject and, especially in your first year at college, you may not know enough or have the experience to decide what is worth marking. Also, if you look at a book for one purpose you could mark things that will not be relevant when you next consult the book – for another purpose. Your earlier marks may then distract and mislead you. It is better to make concise additions to your lecture notes (including relevant page numbers from your textbooks) so that if necessary you can find the same paragraphs quickly if you need them again.

Authors may present information using words, numbers (usually in tables), or in illustrations (diagrams, drawings and photographs), but information presented in one way should not be repeated in another. In reading, therefore, you must study the tables and illustrations as well as the text.

Make notes on wide-lined A4 paper (as used for your lecture notes, see page 64). Begin by recording complete bibliographic details of any publication from which you intend to make notes (as in Figure 7.1). You will need these details if you ever look at this publication again or refer to it in a bibliography or list of references at the end of one of your own compositions

Complete bibliographic details of a paper in a journal are included in Figure 7.1: the author's surname and initials followed by the year of publication (in parenthesis), the title of the article, the name of the journal (underlined in manuscript and either underlined or in italics in typescript), the volume number (underlined with a wavy line in manuscript, and in bold in typescript), the part number (in parenthesis), and the first and last pages covered by the article.

In the complete bibliographic details of a book, the author's surname and initials are followed by the year of publication (in parenthesis), the title of the book (underlined or in italics, as for the name of a journal), the name of the publisher, and where the book was published. For example: GASH, S. (1999) *Effective literature searching for students*, 2nd edn, Gower, Aldershot. For other examples of complete bibliographic details of books, see *Further reading*, pages 209–11).

If you use the name and date method of citing sources, it seems sensible to start the bibliographic details of each source included in your bibliography or list of references with the author's name and the date, but you will find that the order in which bibliographic details is given is not the same in all publications. For you, the most important points are: (a) include complete bibliographic details of each of the publications cited in your composition, and (b) be consistent in the order in which you present these details.

From some pages of a book you may think it worthwhile to make detailed notes, *in your own words*, and to include simple diagrams and flow-charts. However, make sure that your notes on the whole book are concise. Writing out or photocopying long passages, or making detailed notes, may fill your subject files with useless clutter, and so is likely to be a waste of your time. It is better and usually quicker to prepare concise notes and to record page numbers so that you can read important passages from your textbooks several times. In other words, try to store information in your brain rather than on paper. Also remember that your notes are for using, not for storing, and if they are too long they will be of little use either in your studies or in your final revision prior to an examination.

Howe, J. A. (1974) The utility of taking notes
as an aid to learning
Educational Research 16 (3), 222-7

A   The value of note making
       ACTIVITIES

Gather   1. ┌─────────────┐
information   │ CONCENTRATE │
                     └─────────────┘
                Lecturer directs attention.
                2. ┌────────┐
                    │ SELECT │
                    └────────┘
                Student may miss some points
Process   3. ┌──────────┐
information   │ ORGANIZE │
                    └──────────┘
                Arrange to suit your needs
                4. ┌────────┐
                    │ RECORD │ = information
                    └────────┘   and ideas

B   Value of notes later
        Facilitate learning
  ?   BUT notes may contain mistakes
            and misunderstandings.
        Would handouts be better?
        LEARNING is probably related to the
  NB   amount of time given to
        information processing

Figure 7.1 Notes on an article published in a research journal.

Do not make notes as you read for the first time. Start by reading quickly so that you can follow the author's explanations and arguments, see connections, and find the parts which are worth close attention. Then read these parts again, select carefully, and make concise notes (see Figure 7.1). By recording a key word, phrase or sentence about each paragraph, you can reconstruct the author's topic outline (compare Figure 7.1 with Figure 5.2).

If you add your own comments or evaluations, mark them by a vertical line and your initials in the margin. Mark anything that is undecided, or that you question or do not understand, by a vertical line in the margin and a question mark. Make a note, especially, of the answers to your questions or of anything new to you. Later, to clear up any difficulties, use the index or look at other books, or try to find out for yourself, or ask someone who knows, until (if possible) you find the answers to your questions (see page 56).

At the end of each section or chapter, as you read and make notes, stop to *review your progress* (as you would after a lecture, see page 58). Skim through the pages again. Relate the parts to the whole. Check that your notes are accurate and that you have recognised the main points. Add your comments and your evaluation. Devoting time to this review will help you to recall much of what you have read, to understand more, to see connections, and to refresh your memory and so fix in your mind those things that you wish to remember.

Then, for *revision*, try to recall and list the author's main points from memory (see Table 7.2). Check to confirm that you have remembered correctly. Just as before reading you should decide what you want to know (see page 86), so after reading you should check that you have extracted this information.

Making notes is a part of active study which helps you to maintain attention and to think, so that you can select the author's main points, evidence, examples, steps in an argument, and conclusions. In making you think, making notes helps you to understand. Writing is an activity which makes you repeat selected points and so helps you to learn and remember them. You may not remember everything as a result of this first reading, but you can refresh your memory from your notes – without having to read the whole book again. In this way the notes may be useful when you plan an answer to a question set in course work.

Table 7.2 How to read*

Stages in active reading	Activities
1 Survey	*Consider your purpose* What is this composition about? Is it sufficiently up-to-date? Does it contain the information you need?
2 Question	*Ask yourself* Should I read it? If so, which parts should I read? How should I read it?
3 Read critically	*Skim read* selected parts. *Read* again. *Select. Organise* to suit your purpose. *Make notes.*
4 Review	*Consider* what you have read. *Check your notes.* Have you extracted the information you need and arranged it to suit your purpose.
5 Revise	*Remember.* *List* main points from memory.

* Note that this is not the only way to read, but use these suggestions to help you to think about why and how you read, and how you may be able to improve your reading techniques. *Always* define your purpose, read according to your purpose, and read actively – not passively.

One set of notes

Add to or modify your lecture notes in the light of your increased knowledge or better understanding, so that you have only one set of notes on each aspect of your work (see page 167). You may find it helpful to use black ink for your lecture notes and blue ink for other work so that additions can be distinguished easily.

Your notes become an irreplaceable study aid. They provide a framework upon which additional facts and ideas can be hung, so that you can associate this new material with what you already know. This facilitates learning and revision (see Figure 7.2). The value of your notes increases as your course proceeds. They must, therefore, be kept in a safe place. Do not lend them to anyone; and on journeys keep them with you all the time – do not let them out of your sight. You cannot afford to lose the results of one, two or three years' work.

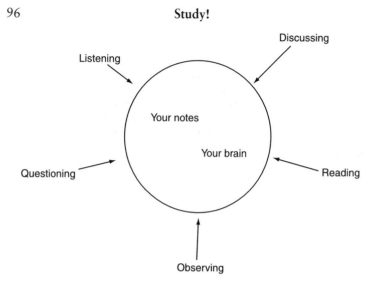

Figure 7.2 The central place of your notes in active study. Sources of information are indicated by arrows. Your notes should be much more than a store: they should be arranged to facilitate collecting, selecting and organising relevant material – as an aid to understanding, learning and revising.

UNDERSTAND AND SELECT

Comprehension tests

Every question set in course work and examinations is a test of your ability to understand. If you do not understand exactly what is required you may answer the wrong question or give an incomplete answer (see pages 110–13). Furthermore, careful reading and comprehension is the first step in making good notes, and in preparing a précis or summary. Teachers who neglect the teaching of comprehension, précis writing and summarising skills, should appreciate that pupils or students who cannot do these things well are handicapped in other aspects of their work.

Writing a précis

In reducing the length of a composition you should omit all figurative language or ornament, anything of secondary importance, and all digressions and superfluous words. With practice you will grasp the essentials of a composition at first reading and writing a précis will become easier.

Regular practice in précis writing will help you to learn aspects of effective study: careful reading and comprehension, the exercise of judgement in selecting the essentials, and accurate reporting. Preparing a précis will also help you to learn more about *selected aspects* of your work. For practice, try writing a précis of a leading article from a good newspaper, an article from a magazine or journal, or one of your own essays. Recognising superfluous words and phrases in other people's work (see pages 121 and 133) will help you to be more critical of your own writing and to develop a more economical and direct style.

Writing a summary

A summary of an article, or of a passage from a book, includes only the main points. It is like a topic outline but is written in complete sentences. Most of your own compositions in course work and examinations will be too short to require a summary. Indeed, an essay should come to some conclusion and should not end with the repetition of points already effectively made (see page 132). However, practice in preparing good summaries (for example of recorded talks and of journal articles) will help you to develop your ability to recognise stages in an argument or topics in a topic outline. It will help you to learn to distinguish quickly between main points and supporting detail (evidence, examples and illustrations).

If you have difficulty in making good notes in lectures, this may be because you try to write too much: you may record too many details yet miss important points. Practice in selecting main points from a composition, when you have more time for thought, will increase your confidence when you have to make notes as you listen in lectures, seminars and tutorials.

If you have difficulty in writing essays and reports, perhaps you include too much detail or perhaps you omit essential points. In your own compositions, as in making lecture notes, you need the confidence to recognise main points and to include only the necessary supporting detail. What you consider to be the essentials, and what is necessary detail, will depend upon why you are writing and for whom you are writing.

If you feel that you are not doing as well as you should in

examinations, perhaps you know the answers but have difficulty in deciding what exactly is required or in organising an effective answer in the time available. Again your difficulty is partly one of selection. Preparing summaries of other people's compositions and topic outlines for your own, will help you to do better work.

Writing summaries of articles, and of important passages from books, should help you to make useful additions to your notes. In this way, as with précis writing, preparing a summary is a method of active study that makes you concentrate, makes you confirm that you understand, and makes you be selective, and so is an aid to learning and remembering.

Some students have difficulty in remembering because they try to remember too much. Except for things that must be remembered word for word (see page 69), rote learning is a waste of time. Practice in preparing summaries should help such students to select only key words and phrases so that they have less to learn. Selection is easy, because in most compositions the first sentence of each paragraph is the topic sentence. Topic sentences and subheadings draw your attention to what the author considers to be the main points. For practice, try writing a summary of an article that includes a summary. Then compare your summary with that prepared by the author.

GET TO KNOW USEFUL SOURCES OF INFORMATION

Information technology is concerned with electronic methods of cataloguing, communicating, processing, storing, retrieving, and publishing information. People speak of the electronic office as a place where there is no need for paper, but much information is still recorded, stored and communicated on paper.

Reference books and journals

Your textbooks may provide all the information you need for a first examination at school, but in more advanced courses and as soon as you begin to think of yourself not as a pupil but as a student, you must learn to make effective use of other books and of other resources available in your college library and in other local libraries. Remember that the librarians are anxious to advise and help if you have any questions about using the library or if you cannot find the information you require (Figure 7.3).

Figure 7.3 The book number in the catalogue will help you to find a particular book, which has this number marked on its spine.

Dictionaries. A good dictionary of the English language that provides a guide to the correct spelling, pronunciation, origin and meanings of each word listed, its function (e.g. n for noun), and its status in the language (see page 136) is an essential reference book for any student (see page 209). Many other dictionaries should be available in the reference section of any good library (including dictionaries of the specialist terms of most subjects, and dictionaries of abbreviations).

For anyone who needs more information than can be included in a desk dictionary, the *Oxford English Dictionary* is a printed multivolume work with CD-ROM and online versions that provide access from a computer terminal to a database comprising more than 500 000 words.

Encyclopaedias. An encyclopaedia, which may be available in a library as a printed multi-volume work or in electronic form via a computer terminal, is a good starting point for anyone coming new to a subject. Each article is written by an acknowledged authority, in language that can be understood by non-specialists, and it ends with references to other sources of information for those who need to know more. Multimedia publications provide spoken words and other sounds as well as printed text, and moving pictures as well as stills. In addition to such general works there are specialist encyclopaedias on many subjects.

Directories. Telephone directories are a useful source of names and addresses, as well as telephone numbers. Other directories provide similar information about, for example, particular trades or professions. Some directories are available in printed and in electronic versions; and some, available only in electronic form are called listings. Access to other sources of constantly up-dated computer-based information is also available by television and via the Internet.

Handbooks. As the name implies, a handbook should be a concise reference book. It provides information on one subject, for day-to-day use (see page 210).

Books. Find out how books are classified in the libraries you use (see Table 7.3). A library's catalogues may be on index cards, or on microfiche, but most large libraries have electronic catalogues accessed from computer terminals. There are printed instructions next to each terminal, and further instructions on the screen at each stage of your search. If you know which book you are looking for, you can search by entering the name of an originator (author, editor or organisation), or the book's title. If you do not have a title or other bibliographic details of a particular book you can search by entering either a subject class number (see Table 7.3) or key words of the kind you would choose when consulting an encyclopaedia of the index of any relevant publication.

When you find a catalogue entry for a book it will include the book's bibliographic details and its classification number (called its book or shelf number). Signs on the library's floor plan and on the

Table 7.3 Three systems for classifying books in libraries

The ten classes of the Dewey Decimal System		Universal Decimal System	Library of Congress System
000	General works	0	A
	Reference books (030)	03	AE
100	Philosophy	1	B
	Psychology (150)	15	BF
200	Religion	2	BL
300	Social sciences	3	H
400	Languages	4	P
500	Pure sciences	5	Q
600	Applied sciences	6	
700	The Arts	7	N
800	Literature	8	P
900	Geography (910)	91	G
	Biography (920)	92	CT
	History (930)	93	C

shelves include both the names of subjects and their classification numbers or letters, as in Table 7.3, to direct readers to the parts of the library in which books on the different subjects are shelved. On each shelf, books on a particular aspect of a subject – with similar book numbers – are arranged in alphabetical order according to the name of the originator (the author, the editor, or an organisation).

Reviews. Some books and journals specialise in the publication of articles reviewing the literature on a particular subject, and some reviews are published in journals that also publish original papers. In a review all relevant published work should be considered, so a review is a good starting point in a literature survey. However, reviews may say nothing of the methods used in the work reviewed and each reference to previous work is necessarily brief and may be misleading. Books and reviews are called secondary sources and it is important to look at original articles (primary sources) to be sure that in referring to the work of other writers you do not misrepresent them.

Journals, magazines and newspapers. Look at the periodicals taken regularly by your library, to see which ones are likely to be of interest to you. Current issues are usually on display, and these may be in a separate room.

Journals that specialise in the publication of original research papers are called primary sources. In these you can read the results of recent work soon after it is published, and see references to related articles that may be of interest.

Articles are not necessarily published in the most appropriate journals, but computer-based information retrieval systems provide easy access to the titles and abstracts of articles in both current issues and back numbers of many journals. A search for articles on a particular subject can be based on key words (words that you would expect to be included in the titles of articles or in journal indices).

There are many thousands of periodicals but most libraries can subscribe to only a few. You should know, therefore, that there are abstracting and indexing journals that help people undertaking a literature search to find articles that are likely to be of interest. Also, many journals that publish original and review articles – and many that publish abstracts, lists of contents of current journals, and indices of key words, are published in electronic as well as print versions, and some only in electronic versions, and these are available via the Internet.

The Internet (World Wide Web)

With a web browser, you can use the web address of a business or other organisation to access its web site from a personal computer and see the pages it provides – which include, for example, words, pictures, videos, plans and maps. Via the Internet, therefore, much useful information is available – but also much unsupported opinion, and much that is fiction.

Unlike the papers published in professional journals (in printed or electronic versions), much of the material on web pages has not been subject to peer review and editing. Also, the contents of web pages may be changed at any time, so readers consulting the same source at different times may not see an identical document. So, keep these reservations in mind when you use the Internet. Also, because web pages may change at any time, if a document is of particular interest you are advised to download it to your computer or to make a hard copy.

Many organisations include a web address on their headed notepaper and in advertisements, and there are directories of web addresses, but if you do not know an address you can try to guess it – because most web addresses comprise: www (the World Wide Web), the name of the organisation (for example ons = Office of National Statistics), an extension indicating the type of organisation (for example com = company; gov = government), and the country (for example uk = United Kingdom) – with full stops where there are commas in this sentence but with no spaces. For example, www.ons.gov.uk is the web address of the Office of National Statistics, a government department in the United Kingdom. However, when you access a web address you must check that the site is that of the organisation you are seeking – because different organisations, perhaps with opposing objectives, may have very similar addresses.

Via the Internet you can also, for example: (a) study previously inaccessible archives, (b) browse through the catalogues of major libraries, (c) scan pages of both current issues and back numbers of newspapers, (d) search indices for bibliographic details and abstracts of publications likely to be of interest to you, and (e) read (and, if necessary, print out or down-load to your computer) articles from journals published electronically (see Table 7.4).

Table 7.4 Some electronic sources of information on articles published in journals

Electronic sources*	Access to
Business Sources Elite	Business, marketing, management and economics journals
Computer database	Articles from computing journals
Emerald	Articles from marketing and management journals
FT McCarthy	Company, industry and market information
INSPEC	Computing and information technology journals and conference proceedings
Sociological Abstracts	Abstracts of articles from sociology journals
Web of Science	Science Citation Index, Social Science Citation Index and Arts & Humanities Citation Index

Note
* As with other businesses and organisations, the names, ownership and location of electronic sources may change.

The Internet also makes available on-line instruction. For example, many of the course materials produced by The Open University in England are available via the Internet, with tutorial support, to students in many countries in Western Europe.

Many individuals have Internet accounts with an Internet Service Provider (ISP), and pay for this either by a direct charge or through a telephone company. Anyone with a personal computer making much use of the Internet will find it expensive, because a search for information can take a long time. You pay directly because of the cost of the service, and indirectly if you value your time. Also: (a) your search will not necessarily be successful, and (b) you will not be able to rely on the relevant material you do find, much of which is likely to be opinion – unsupported by evidence. As when reading books and review articles (secondary sources) you will need to refer to primary sources (see page 102) for the evidence upon which statements are based.

Search engines are used in looking for information on the Internet. Many of these offer both a simple search and a more complex search that may be called an advanced search. However, no search engine could search the whole of the Internet, and if you enter identical search requests into different search engines you will find differences in their outputs even when searching for specialist terms. One reason for these differences is that organisations developing web pages use many different key words, not just the most appropriate words, in an attempt to direct searches to their pages. Another reason is that some search engines accept new web pages quicker than others, and some store pages for longer than others.

Intranets

An Intranet is a web, similar to the Internet, but with restricted access. For example, it may be available within a university – linking computers in different rooms, different buildings and different sites. In an international company an Intranet may link computers in different parts of the world. Because access to an Intranet is restricted the information displayed is easier to control and is likely to be of better quality than much of the information available on the Internet.

OPEN LEARNING

Resources for courses

Some topics, even on full-time courses, may be covered by student centred *open learning* (not in time-tabled classes). Materials provided for private study (for example, work-books and handouts) may be supported by collections of photographs, maps, recordings, tape-slide sets, video tapes and multimedia computer programs (available at college in map rooms, language laboratories and other specialist rooms, or at home via the Internet). There may also be special radio talks and television films (as for Open University courses in the United Kingdom and for similar courses elsewhere). And students have opportunities to discuss problems either in self-help groups or with a tutor, to obtain guidance when necessary, and to check their progress.

Computer-based learning

If your library's catalogues are computer-based, any non-book materials available in the library will be listed – as well as the books. The librarians will also be able to offer advice on computer-based information retrieval. For example, (a) all the information in a multi-volume dictionary or encyclopaedia (see pages 99 and 100) may be available on CD-ROM (Compact Disk Read Only Memory: so called because the user can access but cannot change the information); (b) computer-based multimedia integrates displayed text and diagrams, and photographs, film or video, and sound; and (c) many publications previously available only in book form or as journals, including abstracting and indexing publications (see pages 102 and 103), are now published as an alternative – or instead – on compact disc. As a result, some publications that used to be available only in book form can now be accessed only from a computer terminal.

Computer assisted learning

Computer aided instruction (CAI) gives instruction and then, to test your understanding, gives practice (see *Using your computer*, page 200); and computer aided learning (CAL) provides information, asks you to use this information, and then tests your knowledge and understanding.

Each course begins with a title and a list of things it will help you to do, or help you to learn. Features of these courses are as follows.

1 You can progress at your own pace.
2 You can stop at any point and pick up, later, where you left off.
3 Different approaches to the subject may be provided so that you can choose to learn topics in an order that suits you best (for example, by following on directly from what you already know about the subject).
4 All the instruction is presented on screen (see Figure 7.4).
5 In contrast with traditional learning methods, in which a pen and paper are used, it is usually necessary to type your answers on a keyboard.
6 Your answers appear on the screen.
7 If you make a mistake, you may be able to delete your answer by pressing a key.
8 When you are satisfied with your answer you can press the key which, according to an instruction on the screen, takes you on to the next step if your answer is correct.
9 If your answer is incorrectly entered, your attention is drawn to the mistake. You can then delete letters and make corrections.

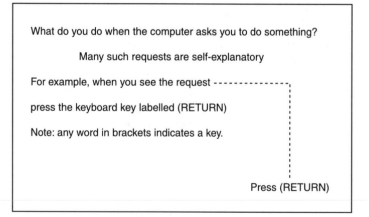

Figure 7.4 Computer Assisted Instruction: words on the screen at one step in a course. Individual programs differ in arrangement.

To summarise, the computer provides the instruction and information, asks questions, evaluates your answers and provides immediate feedback, taking you through the course step by step. This is an active form of learning, because you are made to think (by being given not only information to consider but also questions to answer) and if you do not remember something you can work through part or the whole of the course again.

These programs, like books, vary in quality. To write a good one, the author must know the subject, know how to teach the subject, and know how to program effectively. Do not be put off, therefore, if you do not like the first programs you try.

Except for mathematics questions, in which the computer can check the answer by calculation, the answers to questions set in the program have to be stored in a file. The computer will then accept only this stored answer as correct. If you type in a different but correct answer (e.g. expressing the correct answer in different words) the computer will not recognise it as being correct. To avoid this problem, a question may be presented at the same time as a number of possible answers (as a multiple choice test: see Table 7.5).

Table 7.5 One question from a multiple choice test, as part of a computer assisted learning programme

Computer	Indicate the word which comes closest in meaning to 'Feierabend' in the following sentence.
	Beamte haben einen mehr freizeitbetonten als arbeitsbezogenen Feierabend.
	Type A, B or C: A Freizeit B Zeit nach Arbeitsschluss C Party
Learner	A
Computer	'Freizeit' means 'leisure' or 'free time'. You are looking for an expression with the sense of 'free time after finishing work'.
Learner	B
Computer	That is better. 'Feierabend' has the sense 'free time after finishing work'.

Note 1 The computer can be programmed to guide the learner towards the right answer following a mistake.

2 Table based on Davies, G. (1982) *Computers, Language and Language Learning*, Centre for Information on Language Teaching and Research, London.

A correct answer may then simply be recognised, and you may think you know something that is not yet fixed in your mind. Alternatively, each question may require a yes/no or true/false answer.

As with other sources of information, use computer assisted instruction to complement your standard textbooks, not as a substitute.

8

Write and learn

In discussions, you learn from others and can test your own ideas, but may lose your train of thought or may not have the opportunity to say all that you would have liked to say. In contrast, in private study you can observe, read, contemplate, and then express the results of your thinking. Without interruption, or distraction you can write, correct, revise and if necessary rewrite – until satisfied that this is your best work.

Writing will help you, as a student, to make and record observations, to remember things, to capture thoughts and arrange them in order, and to express your knowledge. It is therefore part of active study. Also, in writing you express yourself. This is why teachers and examiners judge, by your writing in course work and examinations, your knowledge, your understanding, and your ability to organise and communicate thoughts.

In view of the importance of writing in course work and examinations, in applications for employment, and in most professions, consider whether or not your writing could and should be improved. In your writing do you display an educated and lively mind? Does your writing have any of the defects that would cause you to condemn the writing of others (see Table 8.1 and, for examples, page 133)? Does your writing have any of the faults that are commonly encountered by teachers and examiners when they mark students' written work?

FAULTS COMMONLY ENCOUNTERED IN STUDENTS WRITTEN WORK

Because writing is an expression of thought, the faults considered here indicate lack of thought, insufficient thought, or an inability to think clearly.

(a) Lack of knowledge of the subject

The most common reason for poor performance is a failure to display sufficient knowledge of the subject. This may be because the student does not know the whole answer to the question asked, or it may be due to an inability to communicate the information required in an effective answer.

Note and remember those things that the lecturers or tutors who will assess your work obviously consider important. In written work make clear your knowledge and understanding of relevant points emphasised: (a) in the lectures and other organised classes – including field work and other practical work- that formed part of your course, and (b) in any handouts or other self-study material provided to complement your lectures, practical work and tutorials.

You must also make good use of other sources of information, especially the textbooks and other further reading recommended for your course, to fill any gaps in your knowledge or understanding. In course work, when you have time to seek the further information needed to fill such gaps, the regular submission of incomplete answers may be due to lack of ability, to lack of thought and effort, or to lack of organisation and the consequent ineffective use of time.

(b) Lack of understanding

Many students make the mistake of thinking that information is all that is required. Usually the facts of the matter, by themselves, are not enough.

Include enough detail and enough explanation, to show your knowledge and understanding. Define essential terms (especially those used in the question). Summarise evidence and give an example if it will help to make your point. Show your understanding by including only relevant material and by ensuring that your answer is complete and in good order.

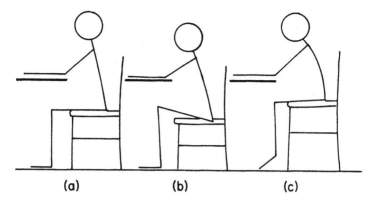

Figure 8.1 If appropriate, include simple diagrams in your compositions. For example: (a) sitting comfortably; (b) and (c) sitting uncomfortably.

Include simple diagrams (see Figures 6.2 and 8.1) if these will contribute to your explanation, help your reader to understand your answer, and help you to give a more complete answer. Place each diagram as near as you can to the part of the answer to which it applies, but number all diagrams and refer to them in your answer (as in this paragraph, and more than once if necessary). Give each diagram a concise caption or legend and use labelling to draw attention to things that are especially relevant to your answer, but do not waste time on shading.

Do not leave things out of your answer because you think they are too elementary. It is best to mention things if they are relevant, even if only in passing. Each question is an opportunity to display your knowledge. The reader cannot guess what you know and you can score marks only for what you write.

(c) Lack of evidence

Statements made in any composition should be supported by sufficient evidence and by appropriate examples. Unsupported statements are unconvincing because they are not easily distinguished from opinions. Also, it is usually necessary for a student to demonstrate knowledge of the evidence for – and against – any statement that might be considered controversial.

Some evidence may come from your own observations but most

will be from the published work of others. Authorities are not necessarily correct in their interpretations of evidence (see page 91) and authority is no substitute for evidence, but sources of any information or ideas that are not your own must be cited. However, note that it is not usual for students to acknowledge the source of what may be regarded as common knowledge (for example, from the introductory textbooks, and from the lectures and other classes that form part of their course).

You must cite other sources of information in your own compositions, and list bibliographic details of these sources (see page 92), for the following reasons.

1 In citing sources you acknowledge your indebtedness to the published work of others.
2 Citing sources helps you to indicate to an assessor that you have done some relevant background reading and are taking more than a beginner's interest in your work.
3 Copying another person's work, if it were the work of another student, would be cheating and would obviously be unacceptable. Similarly, taking extracts from books or other published work and then presenting the words as your own is plagiarism (stealing thoughts) and this too is unacceptable.
4 In course work either a bibliography or a list of the references cited in your composition is necessary, both for your own records and to inform the reader.

In your compositions you may indicate extracts from the work of others by using quotation marks and giving the title of the publication from which the words were taken, the author's name and the date of publication (as on page 79). Note that three dots are used to indicate where some words have been omitted from a quotation; and if any words are added in a quotation these should be within square brackets. Otherwise, all the words and punctuation marks in a quotation must be exactly as used by the author of the work.

Another way to indicate an extract is by indentation (as on page 80) followed by details of the source of the extract. Note that when an extract is presented in this way it is not necessary to use quotation marks.

It is useful to know how to quote from other people's work in your compositions, but in scholarly writing it is more usual to summarise information and ideas that are not your own – taking care not to misrepresent observations, conclusions or views – and then to cite the source of these materials.

One method of citing a source is to insert a number in superscript (or in parenthesis) at the end of a sentence or paragraph, and to list all the sources cited in a composition in numerical order in a bibliography or list of references at the end. However, this numeric system is unsuitable for general use by students because it is not possible to remember complete bibliographic details to list at the end of examination answers.

Another method, which students are advised to use in all their compositions (unless they are citing historical manuscripts or old books that do not include the date of publication), is the name and date system (also called the Harvard system). In this, either the author's surname is followed immediately by the date of publication (in parenthesis) or both the name and the date are in parenthesis at the end of a sentence or paragraph (as on page 135).

In some subjects, especially the sciences and engineering, every composition in course work should end with a *List of references*. This should include complete bibliographic details of all the works cited in the composition, but no others. In other subjects, especially the arts and humanities, works that have influenced your thinking may be included – instead – in a *Bibliography*, even if these have not been cited in your composition.

Look at appropriate books and journals and you will see how sources are cited and how bibliographic details are listed in your subject. Whatever your subject you will find it helpful to look at the British Standard BS 5605 *Citing and referencing published material* (a concise introduction) or for more detail BS 1629 *Bibliographic references* (similar to the International Standard ISO 690).

(d) Lack of logic

Arguments developed within a paragraph, or more usually in successive paragraphs, should lead to a logical conclusion. Logical thought, starting from true premises, leads to a valid conclusion. But thinking illogically, even from true premises, could lead to a valid conclusion only by chance.

(e) Bias

People are inclined to ignore or reject evidence that is contrary to their own preconceived ideas, or evidence that is contrary to what is believed to be currently accepted public opinion (see page 81). However, scholarly writing should be free from bias.

Speculation, if it is necessary, should be clearly indicated by such words as *may, possibly* and *perhaps*. And things first mentioned as possibilities should not later be stated as if they were facts. Nor is it acceptable to go beyond the available evidence: extrapolation is not a reliable method for reaching conclusions. Remember, also, that if two things are correlated it should not be assumed that one is necessarily the cause of the other.

In advertising and politics, for example, it is usual to use emotive language, instead of evidence, and to exaggerate and present only the advantages of a product or selected facts that are in accordance with party dogma. But scholars, seeking the truth, should avoid emotive language and should present evidence for and evidence against – unless they are asked to do otherwise. Where appropriate they should present a variety of opinions, to show that they are aware of different interpretations even if they conclude by supporting one point of view.

(f) Lack of relevance of the whole or part of an answer

Including irrelevant material may be the result of misunderstanding the question, or of a failure to consider exactly what is required (see page 71, pages 136–9), or from digression. Whatever the cause, it is always a waste of time. No marks can be scored for information that is not required. If, therefore, you include anything in your answer that is not obviously relevant, you must make clear why you consider it to be relevant.

Lack of relevance is inevitable if the wrong question is answered. This may happen in course work because the question has been copied incorrectly when dictated in class or from a friend's notes. It may also happen in examinations if a candidate prepares an answer during revision and then is asked a slightly different question (see page 180).

It is a good idea in course work, but a waste of time in examinations, to write the question (the exact words and punctuation marks), when the question is set, at the top of a clean sheet of paper. This same paper can then be used for the first sheet of your answer.

(g) Repetition

Some students write answers which follow closely a lecture on the subject. This is likely to result not only in the inclusion of material that is irrelevant in an answer to a particular question but also in repetition. The techniques of the lecturer are not appropriate for the writer. Unless it is recorded, a lecture can be heard once only. The lecturer may therefore repeat important points for emphasis. For example, the lecture may begin with a statement of the topics to be considered. These will then be discussed in the same order. The important points may finally be included in a brief summary. In writing, however, each main point should normally be made not three times but just once because, if necessary, the words can be read more than once.

(h) Lack of originality

Your answer to a question should be the result of your own thought. An original presentation is not achieved by simply reproducing notes made in a lecture; this course of action is likely to result in an answer that is similar to that of many other students who are taking the same course. Nor is originality achieved by copying appropriate passages from books: apart from other considerations (see page 112) these will be written in different styles and, obviously, none will be your own.

To benefit from lectures, from tutorials and other discussions, from your own observations, and from your background reading (see Figure 5.4, page 75) always think before you consult your notes (see Figure 8.3). Select information that is relevant and answer the questions asked; arrange the material in your own way and *present the results of your own thought.*

An original presentation does not necessarily include original material. As a result of independent thought you may combine ideas and information in new ways to produce new associations and new insights. This is creativity (see also page 117).

BALANCE IS IMPORTANT IN WRITING - AS IN MOST THINGS

Figure 8.2 Carry at least a few sheets of paper and a pen so that you can record interesting observations, bright ideas, or notes of things to do, as they come to mind.

(i) Lack of balance

An unbalanced answer, in which some parts of a question receive too much attention and other parts receive too little, is the result of lack of planning and, in an examination, perhaps also to an inefficient allocation of time (see also Figure 8.2).

(j) Poor organisation

It is not usual to include headings in a literary composition, and at schools pupils may be instructed not to use them in essays written for a teacher of English, but in all subjects it is a good idea to use them at least in planing any composition (see page 72).

In most subjects headings are important in any written work. They help the writer to organise the work, to ensure an effective order of material, to check the relevance of each paragraph to the preceding heading, to avoid repetition, to recognise and avoid distracting side-issues, and to achieve balance and unity. Then headings provide signposts for the reader, concentrate attention on the main points, and make for easy reading -and so for easy marking by an assessor (see page 184). You are therefore advised to use headings in all your written work – unless a particular lecturer has asked you not to do so.

(k) Lack of order – wholeness – unity

When the paragraphs are in an ineffective order this is another sign that the writer did not work to a plan. Words such as therefore, moreover, and however, help the writer to make connections. But without planning such connections cannot be properly made, logical argument is difficult, and an easy flow of ideas is impossible.

WRITE ANSWERS TO QUESTIONS

Creativity

The first stages in composition (thinking and planning) are active study techniques (see page 71).

Before writing you must decide what you wish to say and how best to say it. Listing ideas and preparing a plan (a topic outline) may take a few minutes or several weeks, according to the amount of time that is available or necessary.

In course work start thinking about the question soon after it is set (see page 31). Prepare some notes and a plan for your answer (see page 71) at least a week before you start to write (see Table 3.5, page 33). This will give you time to look for any additional information you require, and to do any necessary background reading. In living with your ideas, you will also have time for second thoughts. By looking for a different approach and a different arrangement of your material, you can make yourself think again and give yourself a basis for choice. As a result you may keep to your first plan, or modify it, or perhaps prefer a new one. You will find that your first thoughts are not always the best. Indeed, most people can benefit by putting their plan on one side for a time and then thinking afresh.

Thinking and making notes – capturing your thoughts before starting to write – is a creative process (Figure 8.3). You use your imagination and your judgement in deciding what to include, how to begin, how to preserve order and make connections, and how to end. As a result of your thought, you put things together in a new way – you make new associations, and gain new insights.

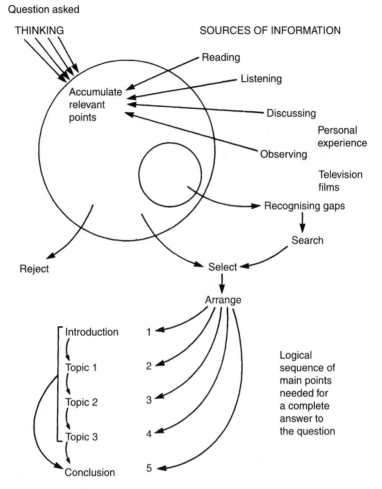

Figure 8.3 Thinking about a question and planning your answer.

As a student you must learn in three ways: (a) by reading or by being told, (b) by finding out for yourself (by observation), and (c) by thinking (considering what you know and making new associations). As you think about your subject things may seem to fall into place. You then achieve a deeper understanding.

In science discoveries are made not only by seeing things for the first time but also, for example, by naming the things observed, and by arranging them in new ways. Observation, naming things, and arranging them, may result in the recognition of order – as in the systems for naming and classifying living organisms devised by Linnaeus in the 18th century, and in the periodic classification of chemical elements proposed by Mendeleyev in the 19th century.

Good ideas come to mind not only when you are working at a task but also when you are relaxing or thinking of other things. Order may then be recognised where previously things seemed only confusing. And the simplicity of this orderly arrangement may be a source of pleasure – as in the simplicity of an efficient engineering construction or a concise mathematical proof.

Most professional writers carry at least a few sheets of paper and a pen so that they can record interesting observations, bright ideas, or notes of things to do, as they come to mind. You are advised to do the same so that you can note, for example, a suitable introduction for a composition you are planning, or an additional topic, or a revised order of paragraphs, or thoughts arising during conversation with lecturers or fellow students. Unless you capture any thoughts that you wish to remember, by making a note, you may find that you cannot recollect them later. It is best to make notes, and to incorporate these at appropriate places in your lecture notes, or in your notes for a composition, at the next opportunity (see page 95).

Making a note is an aid not only to remembering but also to creativity. And with a pencil and paper in your pocket you are ready to write anywhere and at any time. This is one way in which you can make effective use of a few minutes spent waiting for an appointment or half an hour on a bus or train.

Write at one sitting

It is best to write any short composition at one sitting. In examinations you have to do this; and in all written work it is best to get into the habit of writing quickly to maintain the continuity that makes for easy reading.

If you have mastered your subject you will be selective. This, and the need to complete your composition within a word limit (in home-work or other course work) or a time limit (in examinations especially), should help you to avoid verbosity (see page 134).

Descriptive and imaginative writing, and flowery language, which are encouraged at school for some English essays, are not appropriate in answering most questions, especially in other subjects. Your purpose will usually be to explain something – to convey information and ideas. Your writing should not usually be subjective (based on the imagination) but should be objective (based on evidence and supported by examples). It should have the following characteristics: accuracy, clarity, completeness, conciseness, orderliness, and simplicity. Always arrange your thoughts in an effective order and then try to express yourself as clearly and simply as you can.

Write on wide-lined A4 paper and leave wide margins and enough space at the bottom of each sheet (especially the last) for an assessor's comments and corrections.

Use your topic outline as a guide

Most of the faults considered earlier in this chapter are the result of lack of planning. Preparing an outline should help you to avoid these faults, and put you in the right frame of mind for writing. With your topic outline complete, look again at the questions to confirm that your outline does provide the basis for a good answer. Check that you have understood exactly what is required (see Tables 9.2 and 9.3 (pages 138–9); and consider how your answer will be assessed (see Table 8.1). If your outline is a good one it will probably be similar to the marking scheme that will be used in assessing your work. So, write with your outline as a guide.

1 Begin well.
2 Concentrate on one topic at a time.
3 Write quickly.
4 Keep to the point (ensure relevance).
5 Emphasise your main points (topics).
6 Deal with each topic fully in one place.
7 Keep moving at a proper pace, to hold your reader's attention.
8 Avoid repetition.
9 Maintain order.
10 Number tables and diagrams and put each one in the most appropriate place.
11 Make proper connections so that your reader can follow your train of thought.
12 Maintain control.

Table 8.1 Scoring marks for a written answer in a degree course

Standard of work	Mark out of 10	Grade
Outstanding *Presentation.* Work neat, well organised and clearly expressed. *Length* appropriate. *Content.* Displaying knowledge and understanding of all aspects of a complete and correct answer to the question asked. Probably including information and ideas gained by reading beyond standard texts, knowledge of recent work and, for the highest marks, original ideas.	8+	A
Good Displaying knowledge of most or all aspects of a complete answer, but understanding not always made clear, and perhaps giving no indication of background reading. Perhaps longer than is necessary and including some irrelevant material.	6+	B
Average *Answer incomplete*: does not include all essentials. Unnecessary repetition and *poor organisation* may indicate an incomplete grasp of the subject, or an inability to communicate effectively. May include *irrelevant material*, indicating that the question was not properly understood.	5	C
Just acceptable	4	D
Answer inaccurate or incomplete. Not up to the required standard.	3	F
Displaying little knowledge and no understanding.	2	F
Displaying no knowledge or including only irrelevant material.	0	F

13 Ensure completeness and coherence – wholeness – unity.
14 Arrive at an effective conclusion.

CRITICISE THE WORK OF OTHER WRITERS

You can learn to criticize your own compositions, and then improve them, by first looking critically at the work of others. For example, consider the following extracts from a book on study skills.

> It generally takes longer to say something than to read it. It has been estimated for example that the main news bulletin contains less words than a page of *The Times*. Broadcasts therefore have to be even more selective than newspapers. In the case of television, pictures as well as words have to be selected.
>
> Television news ... is supposed not to have an editorial stance; ... to be objective and uncommitted – to be balanced. However, this is in itself a particular stance, which is all the more powerful because of its air of disinterested authority. How far news programmes can be uncommitted is a matter of argument. Lord Reith, the first Director General of the BBC, once said that the BBC could never be neutral between right and wrong – and everyone's ideas of what is right and wrong differ to some degree.
>
> Just as newspapers have journalists and editors, so broadcasting has scriptwriters, producers and programme planners. What is shown, what it sounds like, depends on their decisions.
>
> *Preparing to Study*, Open University (1979)

Thoughts of a critical reader

Paragraph 1 Comments

1 Is *generally* the right word? Would *usually* be better?
  Is *less* the right word? Would *fewer* be better?
2 Does the main radio news bulletin last for 10 minutes or 30 minutes?
  How long does it take to read every word on a page of *The Times*?
  Does the second sentence provide evidence or an example illustrating the point made in the first sentence? If not, does this mean that the first sentence is incorrect?

3 Strictly it is not the broadcast or the newspaper that is selective but the scriptwriter or editor.

4 Would it be better, instead of the verbose phrase *In the case of television* to write *For television*? Is it always better, instead of using the words *in the case of* to say what you mean?

Paragraphs 2 and 3 Points for discussion.

5 Because people differ in their opinions about what is right or wrong, can any scriptwriter or producer be disinterested?

6 Because scriptwriters and editors have to be selective, only some facts relating to an occurrence can be passed on to the readers. How do you think they decide what to tell you? Should they tell you only the things they expect you to want to know?

See how others write

Study leading articles in good newspapers, and articles in magazines that are relevant to your course of study. Ask yourself these questions.

> Does the title capture my interest?
> Does the first sentence make me want to read further?
> Is each paragraph relevant? Pick out the topic sentence of each paragraph and reconstruct the author's topic outline.
> Are the paragraphs in an appropriate order?
> Do they lead to an effective conclusion?
> Are the arguments convincing?
> Are all your questions answered?

When you have reconstructed the author's topic outline, for any short article that is of interest to you, put the article on one side and then write an article yourself, based on this topic outline. Then compare the two compositions. In this way you will learn more about your subject and you will practise writing. Is your composition as interesting and as easy to read as the original? Repeating this exercise with different short articles, or with extracts from books, will help you to develop your ability to pick out key points, to consider how others organise and present their material, and to develop your own style of writing.

CHECK YOUR OWN WORK

In an examination, check each answer immediately, as you complete it (if you have time) and check all your answers again at the end of the examination to ensure that there are no major omissions and to correct obvious mistakes.

In course work you have more time for each of the four stages in composition, so always think, plan, write and then check your work (see Table 3.5, page 33). You will find it helpful to put a composition on one side for at least a few days, when you think it is complete, and then look at it afresh – checking for both content and presentation.

You may think that content is all important, and that marks should not be deducted for mistakes in spelling, punctuation and grammar, or for other defects in presentation. But even if an assessor does not deduct marks for poor presentation, a student misses opportunities to gain marks if the assessor is unable to appreciate the student's knowledge and understanding because thoughts are not expressed clearly, concisely, simply, convincingly and forcefully – all of which depend on good presentation. So, to score good marks for written work you must take care not only with what you write (content) but also with how you write (presentation). See Table 8.2 for a check list that will help you to ensure that all your written work is well presented.

You should not get into the habit of writing things more than once; but if you have spent several hours preparing and writing an assignment you should be prepared to reconsider it to see if you can improve it – in an attempt to score higher marks.

If you need to revise your work this does not mean that you are unintelligent. On the contrary, with further thought an intelligent person should be able to improve a first draft. As in editing someone else's work, creativity is involved in checking, criticising and revising your own compositions. You may recognise irrelevance or illogicality, or decide upon a better arrangement.

HOW COURSE WORK MARKS AFFECT YOUR GRADES

In many colleges both course work and examination marks contribute to assessment. That is to say, students are judged not just by their performance over a few days in examinations but also by their

Table 8.2 Checking a composition in course work

Content: *what you have written*

1 Do your main points stand out?

2 Have you explained each main point sufficiently? Would an example help the reader?

3 Is each statement accurate and based on sufficient evidence?

4 Are your sources acknowledged?

5 Is your composition unbiased, and are any opinions clearly indicated as such?

6 Have you included any imprecise words (for example, few, many, some, several, large and amall) that could be replaced by a number or a number and a unit of measurement?

7 Are any technical terms, symbols or abbreviations you have used: (a) needed, and (b) sufficiently explained?

8 Have you paid the right amount of attention to each part of the question? Is your composition as a whole well balanced?

9 Is every sentence relevant?

10 Is your composition a complete answer to the question set?

Presentation: *how you have written*

11 Is every sentence clearly expressed?

12 Are there any superfluous words, phrases, sentences or paragraphs that will distract the reader's attention from your message?

13 If your work is hand-written, is every word legible?

14 Can you find any mistakes in spelling, punctuation or grammar? It is better to correct them yourself, if you can, than to lose marks because your meaning is not clear or because of the poor impression created in the mind of the assessor.

15 Are your paragraphs in an effective order? Does each one lead smoothly to the next?

16 Have you included appropriate signposts (headings or letters) to indicate the parts of your answer relating to the different parts of the question set?

17 Are your arguments arranged logically and your conclusions stated clearly?

18 Have you numbered any tables or figures (diagrams) separately, and referred to each of them at least once in the text?

19 Are all the sources cited in your composition, but no others, included in a *List of references* at the end of your composition; or have you included a *Bibliography*?

20 Have you underlined words that should be underlined (but no others) or printed them in italics, namely: titles of publications, names of genera (for example, *Homo*) and names of species (for example, *Homo sapiens*) and any words from another language that are not accepted as English words (for example, *in loco parentis*)?

21 Have you kept within the word limit stated when the question was set?

22 Does your answer read easily and does it sound well when read aloud?

---

effort (or lack of effort) over the whole year – as indicated by their marks for homework, practical work, and other assessed course work. This is an advantage to those students who find it difficult to cope with anxiety prior to examinations, and is helpful to any student why feels unwell immediately preceding or during one or more examinations. But fair assessment of course work presents problems, including the following.

1 A question set in course work should be an aid to learning. The students should learn not only from preparing the composition but also from an assessor's comments and corrections. If the mark awarded contributes to the assessment, the student becomes more interested in knowing the mark and so less interested in any feedback. Aspects of teaching (the assessor's comments) become part of the assessment, so the student is assessed before having had the opportunity to learn from these comments.

2 A disadvantage with continuous assessment, in which students are assessed while they are still learning, is that marks awarded indicate not how students have benefited from the course as a whole but what they knew and understood – or what they did not yet know or understand – at the time they prepared the assignments for assessment. If the whole point of education is to teach students to think and help them to achieve their full potential, then the advantage of assessment solely by means of final examinations (at the end of the course) is that students are then in a position to have benefited from their earlier mistakes and from the course as a whole.

3 When work is done in other than examination conditions it is not possible to know how much help a student has received. Cheating and plagiarism are possible and may not be detected.

An examination is an attempt to ensure that all students are tested at the same time and under similar conditions. The marks awarded, therefore, are usually considered to provide a more reliable indication of a student's ability in academic subjects than do course-work marks. This is why, in calculating the total mark for each aspect of the work, tested in an examination paper and in related course work, the examination mark usually contributes more than the course work mark to the final mark.

Table 8.3 Contribution of course work and examination marks to
assessment in each course unit or module

	Course units			
	1	2	3	4
Student W				
Course work	68	64	64	60
Examination	64	59	47	69
Total*	65	61	52	66
Student X				
Course work	62	59	63	56
Examination	32	38	39	50
Total*	41†	44	46	52
Student Y				
Course work	53	50	57	53
Examination	43	42	55	46
Total*	46	44	56	48
Student Z				
Course work	20	38	57	42
Examination	47	65	57	58
Total*	39	57	57	53

Notes * The total for each course unit is calculated as 30% course work mark plus 70% examination mark.
  † This student may fail in this unit, in spite of good course work, because the examination
  mark is so low.

Students should know, from the start of their course, how they
will be assessed. If both course work and examination marks
contribute to the final mark, they should know how this final mark
for each unit is calculated (for example, 30% course work mark
plus 70% examination mark, see Table 8.3).

Students who do not complete assessed course work exercises
deprive themselves of practice and of opportunities for learning (see
page 71); and they cannot benefit from the assessors' corrections and
suggestions. If course work marks do contribute to the final assessment, the consequences of not handing in course work should be
considered. Note, for example, that an obviously capable student
(for example student C in Table 8.4) may fail in course work,
whereas a weaker but better organised student (for example student

Table 8.4 Scoring marks for course work

| Student | Marks out of 20 for five course work exercises | | | | | | Course work Result |
	1	2	3	4	5	%	
A	12	13	9	10	NS	= 44	Pass
B	10	NS	8	6	10	= 34	Fail
C	14	NS	NS	10	12	= 36	Fail
D	8	8	7	10	9	= 44	Pass

NS, work not submitted for marking.

D in Table 8.4) may pass. Note also that a student who obtains poor course work marks, even with satisfactory examination marks, may fail to achieve a pass in this aspect of the work (for example student Z in Table 8.4).

WRITING AND LEARNING

Most of your compositions at school and college (and afterwards) are prepared for other people. However, consider their value to yourself.

1 Thinking and planning, as part of active study (see page 71) are aids to learning. You review one aspect of your work as you think and plan, deciding what should or should not be included. You recognise gaps in your knowledge and then try to fill them.
2 Each composition is a vehicle for self-expression. You will feel satisfaction when the work is complete.
3 If your work has been done thoroughly you will feel that writing has increased your understanding.
4 Compositions are required, in course work, not only as a means of monitoring your progress and assessing your work but also to give you regular practice in expressing your thoughts clearly and concisely (as you will have to do in examinations).
5 Preparing a composition helps you to view your own progress and to benefit from a reader's comments.
6 Thinking and planning encourage creative activity (see page 117), which is a source of pleasure. You organise your thoughts and then, in writing, you present ideas and information *in your own*

way. You ensure that your composition is original in approach, content and arrangement. No one else would, for example, select the same material for inclusion, make the same criticisms, decide upon the same arrangement, or reach the same conclusions.

When you submit course work for assessment do you: (a) write the question in full, your name and the date; (b) submit a topic outline or plan with your answer; (c) write one paragraph on each topic; (d) arrange your paragraphs in an effective order; (e) include enough explanation and perhaps an example in each paragraph; (f) use diagrams if these will help the reader and reduce the number of words required; (g) include appropriate headings to direct attention to each aspect of your answer; (h) cite sources; and (i) list complete bibliographic details of all sources cited (but no others)?

When assessors mark your work do you expect them to: (a) write legibly; (b) correct mistakes, misconceptions and misunderstandings; (c) correct mistakes in spelling, punctuation and grammar; (d) comment on the length of your composition; (e) draw attention to aspects given insufficient attention, to any omissions, and to irrelevant material; (f) include advice to help you improve your methods of working and your communication skills; (g) refer you to other sources of information; (h) offer further tutorial help if they consider it necessary; and (i) encourage you to strive to achieve your full potential?

Consider carefully any feedback on your assessed course work. Learn from your assessors' comments and suggestions, which are intended to provide further instruction and encouragement – and should help you to improve your work. If you are still unable to understand any comment, after thinking carefully and consulting your notes and books, ask the assessor for help. Then file your marked work with your lecture notes on this aspect of your studies. To benefit further from your experience in preparing this composition, amend your lecture notes where necessary and, perhaps, revise your topic outline.

There is no harm in discussing relevant points with a fellow student before you write a composition but close collaboration is obviously unacceptable. Unless instructed to do otherwise you must always prepare your own topic outline, to ensure an original approach, and then write alone.

However, after set work has been assessed, much is to be gained by looking carefully at the work of students whose marks are higher than your own. The best of these may serve as specimen answers – indicating what is required by your teachers from students on your course. You may find that their work contains fewer mistakes, or includes only relevant information and ideas, or is better organised and more complete. Considering these differences, and any comments on your own assessed work, should help you to recognise your strengths and weaknesses and to improve your next composition.

9

Express yourself

A command of language provides the basis for learning: words enable you to think and to express your thoughts. The more words you know, therefore, the better are you able to express yourself. However, communicating your thoughts unambiguously, so that you cannot be misunderstood, is not just a matter of choosing the right words.

WRITING ABOUT YOUR SUBJECT

To express yourself clearly in writing, with no help from facial expressions or other gestures, your words must be effectively arranged in sentences. This is why grammar, the art of using words correctly in an appropriate context, is important in any language.

If you plan to be a scientist or engineer, and think that clear writing and the correct use of language are more important for students of arts subjects than for you, be assured that this is not so. Scientists and engineers must be able to conduct investigations and to communicate their results. They are expected to work with precision – and communication is part of their work.

Whatever your subject, if you need help with your writing, the advice given in this chapter should help you to avoid those mistakes in the use of language that are most commonly encountered in students' written work.

Write in paragraphs

Because each paragraph is concerned with one topic, your paragraphs will vary in length. However, it is probably best in course work and examinations if no paragraph is too long. If the topics in your composition are of comparable importance, your paragraphs will probably be similar in length – contributing to a balanced whole.

Effective paragraphing helps you to arrange topics in an appropriate order, to avoid digression, to give a complete answer, and to hold your reader's attention and interest.

In an essay-type answer your first paragraph should introduce the subject. You should normally make clear, by your use of words from the question, that you do understand what is required and that you have begun to answer the question (see page 72). Each paragraph should be signposted by starting a new line and by indentation, and should be concerned with a distinct part of your answer (one topic). The first sentence should normally be the topic sentence which indicates clearly what the paragraph is about, and this should help you to keep to the point.

Use the first words of each paragraph to convey information: these first words make most impact upon the reader. This is especially important for a student in trying to score marks by adding to what has already been said. However, if you think it will help your reader to see each of your main points, do number your paragraphs or use effective subheadings (as in a magazine or newspaper article). Your first words will then help you to grasp the reader's attention and to score marks.

Short answers to questions, occupying only a few pages of writing, do not normally require a summary. Additional marks should not be given for repeating things that have already been marked. It is best to use your final paragraph to say something more. It should not be a summary but an effective conclusion that follows naturally from, and draws together, your preceding paragraphs.

Write in sentences

Even when you are making notes it is best to use either single words and phrases, to serve as reminders, or to write concise but carefully constructed sentences. If words and punctuation marks are missing, for example from arguments, explanations or definitions, you may not be able to understand your notes when you refer to them some time later.

Similarly, in course work and examinations, readers are most likely to understand complete and properly constructed sentences. If you have difficulty in expressing thoughts clearly and simply, you are advised to write in short sentences and to use each sentence to express just one thought.

What is wrong with each of the following sentences?

1 He only made one journey which aroused the interest of detectives.
2 Only one in seven candidates is accepted because of bad spelling.
3 After the speeches ... the two youngest boys received momentums.
4 It is my pleasure to thank the ladies who helped to serve the refreshments, which included two young girls.
5 Mrs Clay gave a demonstration on China painting, and some members painted themselves.
6 If we imagine a student on a three-year course who reads eleven hours per week during ten-week terms but never during vacations nor at any time in the rest of his life, he would need to make less than 3 per cent improvement in reading efficiency after thirty hours' tuition before we could say that the time spent training him to read faster was not saved by increased efficiency.
7 Naturally, the postal courses which have been in existence the longest must be the best, otherwise they would not have survived so long.

Some comments

1 The word 'only' is out of place. The author presumably intended to write not that *he made only one journey* but that *only one of his journeys* aroused the interest of detectives.
2 The meaning intended here is that six out of seven candidates are rejected because of their bad spelling.
3 Malopropisms, which result from confusing words that are similar in sound or spelling (e.g. momentum and momento), are

named after Mrs Maloprop, a character in Sheridan's *The Rivals* who confused many words (e.g. contagious for contiguous).

4 The speaker intended to thank the ladies who, helped by two young girls, had served the refreshments.

5 Here again events are incorrectly reported as a result of lack of care in writing the sentence.

6 The meaning of these 71 words, which begin with a capital letter and end with a full stop, is difficult to grasp. There are too many negatives: *never . . . nor* (which should read *never . . . or*) and the clumsy phrase *not saved by increased*. The writer's intended meaning can be conveyed clearly, more forcefully, and positively, in 42 words, as follows.

In three years at college a student who reads for eleven hours a week, in term time only, would need an improvement in reading efficiency of as little as 3 percent to more than offset thirty hours spent on a reading course.

7 Only one course can be the best. Also, the evidence given does not support this illogical statement. A new course could be the best.

Take an interest in words

Learning any new words, and practice in using them correctly in sentences, will improve your command of language. You are advised, therefore, to have a good dictionary on your bookshelf (see page 209).

However, a more common fault in writing than the use of the wrong word is the use of a long word when a short one would be better (for example, commence, fabricate, importantly, individuals and utilise – instead of begin, build, important, people and use); and the use of more words than are needed to convey a message pleasurably (e.g. actual facts, green in colour, and I myself would hope – instead of facts, green, and I hope). Superfluous words are obstacles to efficient communication and so are more than a waste of your reader's time.)

Use enough words for your purpose: neither too few nor too many. Most readers will be impressed not by long words (Figure 9.1) or by an excess of words but by relevant information and good ideas clearly and simply expressed. Just as practice enables a golfer to complete a course in fewer strokes, so practice enables a writer to develop a more direct and simple style. In golf you try to go round a

PREFER THE SHORT WORD UNLESS A LONG WORD
WILL SERVE YOUR PURPOSE BETTER

Figure 9.1 To be able to study at home may be an advantage depending upon your circumstances.

course in as few strokes as possible, but the ball must be put in one hole before you can proceed to the next. Similarly, in writing, practise an economy of words but use enough to convey your meaning. Also, help readers to follow your argument by making proper connections between sentences and paragraphs.

Arthur Quiller-Couch (1916) in his lectures *On the Art of Writing* and George Orwell (1946) in an essay on Politics and the English Language gave what is still good advice for those who wish to use language to express and not to conceal their thoughts. Prefer the active to the passive verb (for example, prefer 'The teacher questioned him' to 'He was questioned by the teacher'. Prefer a concrete noun (the name of something you can touch or see) to an abstract noun (for example, area, character, field, nature, situation, and type). Prefer the direct word to the circumlocution (for example, prefer *now* to *at this precise moment in time*). Prefer the fresh turn of phrase to the cliché (for example, instead of writing 'I cannot see the wood for the trees', choose words that convey your meaning precisely). Prefer the short word to the long one (for example, prefer *about* to *approximately*, unless you do mean very closely). Be positive (especially, avoid double negatives such *not unlikely*). And avoid specialist terms, unless you are writing only for specialists.

Write in standard language. Although colloquial language and slang may be used in conversation, and in correspondence between close friends, they should not be used in course work and examinations (except when quoting using exact words and punctuation marks). Colloquial and slang words are marked in a dictionary by abbreviations (colloq. and sl.), so consult a dictionary if you think a word may not be acceptable in your written work.

Colloquial language includes the shortened forms of certain words, in which missing letters are replaced by an apostrophe. In your course work and examinations prefer *do not* to *don't*, *will not* to *won't*, *cannot* to *can't*, and never write it's.

The words used in questions. One of the most common faults in students' course work and in examinations is a failure to answer precisely the question asked. Your first step in preparing any answer in course work or in examinations, must be to consider carefully the precise wording of the question and the meaning of each word used (see page 137). What exactly does your reader want to know?

In examinations you must allow at least a few moments for a relaxed but careful consideration of any question before you plan your answer. However, while you have time, consider the meaning of the words that are commonly used in the questions set in course work and examinations, for example:

> account, analyse, assess, brief, calculate, comment, compare, consider, contrast, criticise, define, describe, detailed, discuss, enumerate, essay, evaluate, explain, general, how, illustrate, interpret, justify, list, opinion, outline, prove, relate, review, state, summarise, trace, and view.

In advanced courses, especially, questions are set to test not only your ability to remember what you have studied but also your understanding. Therefore, you are less likely to be instructed to *describe* something than, for example, to *criticise, discuss, evaluate,* or *outline*. To do such things well you must have mastered your subject, be able to distinguish main points from supporting detail, and be willing to answer precisely the question asked. You are unlikely to be asked to write all you know about a subject. Instead

Table 9.1 Some instructions used in questions and their meanings

Instruction	What you are expected to do
Criticise	Judge the merit of a work, person, statement, or thing. Include points in favour as well as against.
Describe	Give a description in words (and perhaps including a diagram) so that the reader can form an idea of an object, sensation, incident etc. Is your opinion required?
Discuss	Draw attention to all aspects of the question, consider different views and interpretations, and any applications.
Evaluate	Balance evidence for and against, and then give your opinion in the light of this evidence.
Illustrate	Include a diagram or give a definite example (depending upon the context).
Outline	Indicate the limits or scope of your answer; include main points only (not details). What? Where? When? How? Why? Who?

the words of the question will indicate clearly just what is required. As in all writing the most important consideration is not what you would like to tell the reader but what the reader wants or needs to know (for example, see Table 9.1).

If told to discuss you must present a reasoned discussion of the evidence that bears upon the question – not unsupported opinions. If you have to explain the difference between process A and process B do not simply describe A and then B. If asked to compare things you must also contrast them. If instructed to write an essay you must do so; but understand that an answer in a written examination should not necessarily be in essay form. If asked to define a term you must give a carefully considered definition (see page 139). If asked for *either* . . . *or* . . . do not do both. If asked to answer in a certain number of words, do not write more. If asked to list items, do make a list – in an appropriate order – but do no more unless another instruction indicates that more is required. If asked for an annotated diagram only, provide no more.

Unless you consider carefully the meaning of each word used in a question, you are unlikely to give a complete or correct answer. As a result you will not score all the marks available. It is worth undertaking a four-part analysis of any question before planning your answer (see Tables 9.2 and 9.3).

Table 9.2 Thinking about the words used in a question

Question Make brief notes on the difficulties encountered in making observations; and then explain why observation is important in science.

Four part analysis of question*
1 Subject matter
    Observation

2 Aspect of subject matter
    (i)   *Difficulties*
    (ii) *Importance in science*

3 Restriction/expansion of subject matter
    Brief notes (not an essay) on difficulties
    (not on methods or other aspects)
    Why observation is important *in science*
    Note that the words of the question tell you what is required and this should cause you to omit aspects of your knowledge of the general subject area that are not relevant to this question.

4 Instructions
    Make brief notes
    then explain

Plan of answer
1 *Difficulties encountered in making observations*
    (i)   *Inadequate preparation*
    (ii–v) see pages 78–82 for subheadings.
    Write brief notes only below each subheading: enough to indicate that you do understand the difficulty.

2 *Importance of observation in science*[†]
    (i)   Science is *knowledge*: new observations are additions to knowledge.
    (ii) Scientists observe things that they do not understand; they recognise these as *problems*.
    (iii) Problems may be stated as questions; and *hypotheses* are possible answers.
    (iv) Observations made to obtain further *evidence* bearing upon the problem.
    (v)   Experiments made to *test* hypotheses: observations recorded as *data*. The analysis of data yields results.
    (vi) Published observations may be *starting point* in work of other scientists.

---

* Remember the initial letters S A R I (1) Subject, (2) Aspect, (3) Restrictions, (4) Instructions.
[†] See also Figure 5.3 (page 74).

Table 9.3 Thinking about the words used in another question

Question Give an account of population growth in England in the 18th century.

Analysis of question

1 Subject matter
   Population

2 Aspect of subject matter
   Growth

3 Restriction/expansion of subject matter
   (i) England (not Britain or United Kingdom)
   (ii) In 18th century (not 17th, 19th or 20th century)
   Note that the words of the question tell you what is required and, therefore, remind you of what is not required.

4 Instructions
   Give an account

Plan of answer
   Population of England in 1700
                    and in 1800
   Growth of towns/rural population
   Immigration/emigration: effect on population size.
   Possible reasons for population growth in England.
   Conclusion, including reference to other countries: world perspective.

The words of your subject. Every subject has its own technical terms: the words that are peculiar to the subject, or used in a special sense.

These words are used in your textbooks but they may not be fully explained or sufficiently defined. You may have to look at more than one book to make sure that you understand the meaning of each term that is new to you. Unless you know these words you will be handicapped in your studies and you may not understand some questions in examinations.

Show your understanding of the technical terms of your subject by using them correctly and, when you are asked to do so, by giving a precise and complete definition.

Definitions. The best way to make yourself think about the meaning of any term is to try to define it, correctly and completely but concisely. Also, some examination questions start with the word define. You must therefore, consider carefully what a definition is.

In a definition you must start by stating the general class to which the thing to be defined belongs and then proceed to its particular characteristics. For example, of the kinds of words used in a language, you might start defining a noun by saying that it is a word. It belongs to the general class of things called words. But what kind of word is it? How do you recognise a noun? You need a definition that would enable anyone to distinguish this kind of word from any other – such as a verb.

When you prepare a definition, first note the points that must be included, as if you were preparing a topic outline for an essay. Then write your definition. It should be as simple as possible and yet must cover all instances of the thing defined. Note that the definition does not include examples, but it is usually followed by an example or by examples.

> A noun is *a word that is the name of a thing*, such as a person, a place, an object, or an emotion.

Preparing a definition that is as simple as possible but complete and accurate, is an aid to learning. This is probably the only way for you to test that you do understand fully the words of your subject. It should be a regular part of active study.

Check your written definitions by consulting a dictionary and your textbooks. You may find, even in textbooks, that different authors give different definitions of the same term: perhaps some are incomplete. If, after thinking about a word carefully, you are not sure that your definition is correct, discuss the term with a lecturer.

Avoid abbreviations. The use of abbreviations saves time in note-taking (see Table 4.1, page 51) but it is best to avoid abbreviations in assessed work, if you can, and to explain any necessary abbreviation (in parenthesis) the first time you use it.

Abbreviations that are so well known as to require no explanation must be used correctly. Some students indicate that they do not know the meaning of the abbreviations e.g. (L. *exempli gratia*: for example) and i.e. (L. *id est*: that is) by using one when they should be using the other.

The abbreviation etc., at the end of a list (as on page 169), indicates only that the list is incomplete. It is usually better to write the words *including* or *for example* immediately before the list.

Write regularly and read good prose

Part of your long-term preparation for answering the kinds of questions you will be set in examinations (see page 71), which will also result in better course work marks than could otherwise be possible, is to prepare and write answers to questions regularly throughout your course – even if homework is not set regularly.

The easiest way to overcome any reluctance to put pen to paper and to ensure regular practice in composition, is to correspond regularly with a friend or relative. This provides opportunities for self-expression, if each letter is considered and has a beginning, a paragraph for each topic, and a suitable conclusion. Pleasure comes from writing your letters and from receiving replies.

The way we speak is influenced, usually subconsciously, by the speech we hear. Similarly, our ability to write good English can be improved by reading good English regularly. Reading, also, is a source of enlightenment and pleasure. If you read a newspaper, take one that is well written, interesting, and suitable for a person of your intelligence. Also, read well-written books by authors who know how to capture your attention and maintain your interest.

Write legibly

Clear handwriting makes for easy communication, and so contributes to efficiency and is good manners. If a word is necessary you will want people to be able to read it. Words that cannot be read convey no meaning and so, for a student, can score no marks – but they do create an unfavourable impression. If necessary, therefore, try to improve your handwriting for *legibility and speed.*

Letters should not be so small that they are hard to read, nor so large that there is no space between the lines of writing. And the gap between words should not be so small that the words merge, nor so large that the spaces instead of the words capture the reader's attention.

With your paragraphs in mind, write in whole sentences – not thinking of one word at a time. Therefore, form letters so that each word can be written quickly. Legibility is important but a laboured neatness is more than a waste of time: slow handwriting holds back your train of thought and, if time is limited, reduces the number of thoughts that you can express.

Unlike slow reading (see page 89), slow writing is a handicap for a student. Children learn to read one letter at a time, and in learning to write they must, of course, print each letter separately. Many slow writers continue to do this: they do not progress from printing to *real* writing. If you form each letter separately but would like to write faster, practice forming patterns, connected letters, and whole words, without lifting your pen from the page before the end of a line or the end of a word. As you write, complete each word before raising your pen from the paper to cross t's and dot i's, and to proceed quickly to the next word – until rapid writing is a habit.

Whatever you write, leave adequate margins and do not break words between lines: if there is not enough space for the whole word at the end of one line, start the word on the next.

Set yourself speed tests. Write something that you wish to learn by heart (see page 69). Write it again and again, as a writing speed test, until you know the words. Repeat this exercise with other things that you must learn.

For all assessed work use black or blue-black ink, so that (i) there is sufficient contrast between your words and the page, and (ii) your writing cannot be confused with the markers' comments and corrections.

TALKING ABOUT YOUR SUBJECT

Talking in tutorials and seminars (see page 59) provides good practice and helps you to gain confidence in speaking in public, as you will have to do in any career when participating in meetings. In studying most subjects you will probably also have opportunities to give short talks to other students.

Preparing a short talk (or presentation)

To give a good talk you need to know your subject and to be well prepared. When asked to give a talk you need to know: (a) what you are to speak about, (b) to whom you will be talking, (c) how many minutes have been allowed for your talk, (d) the date and time at which you will be expected to speak, and (e) where you will be giving your talk and what facilities will be available for you to use. It is also important to know the size of the room and the likely size of the audience. As a student you are most likely to be talking to a small group of students, in the presence of a tutor, and in familiar surroundings.

You are likely to be given a title for your talk, and to have the opportunity to discuss the purpose and scope of your talk with a tutor. Alternatively, you may be given concise terms of reference. As in writing, the first step in preparing a talk is to think about the title or terms of reference, and to remember that the most important consideration is what your listeners need to know. List a number of important points and then number them in an effective order. You may need to look for further information. Then it is a good idea to write out your talk in full, but to speak from concise notes.

Most inexperienced speakers try to make too many main points and to support their arguments with too much detail. By writing out a talk and reading it aloud to yourself you can check that you have not written things that you would not say, and that you have not tried to say more than is possible in the time available.

One reason why you cannot say as much in a talk as you could read aloud in the same time is that speech is not the same as writing. Repetition, which is usually undesirable in writing, is essential in a talk. You should begin by saying what you are going to talk about, perhaps giving a clearer indication of the scope of your talk than can be gained from the title. Then you must make each of your main points, briefly rephrasing each statement to ensure everyone understands each stage of your talk. Then you will probably summarise, repeating each of your main points so that you can come to your conclusion.

In a twenty-minute talk people should not find it difficult to maintain attention. In a longer talk, people will listen carefully to and remember best what you say in the first fifteen minutes; and thirty minutes with one person talking is enough for any listener. A well planned talk may therefore follow this sequence: brief introduction – main points – examples and elaboration supported by visual aids to provide a change in the medium of communication – conclusions – questions and discussion.

As a student you are likely to be asked to talk for ten to twenty minutes about a topic that is part of your course. You must relate the number of main points to be made to the time available, the needs of other students who will probably be taking notes, and the time needed to introduce the subject, to use visual aids, and to end the talk effectively.

Some speakers underline key words in their notes and mark the margin to indicate where they should be at different times. Others use index cards, with one for the introduction, one for each main point, and one for the conclusions. And others use slides or overhead projector transparencies, so that each main point appears on a screen and serves as a reminder – but this may result in the speaker looking at the screen instead of at the audience.

If you use cue cards, then speak from memory as you would in conversation, this should help you to move forward at a pace that is suited to your audience. Remember that, in listening, the audience also need time to look at your visual aids and they may also need the pauses readers get from punctuation marks, paragraph breaks and new headings. Remember that, in speaking, one way to make an important point is to use a visual aid, another is by a change of voice, and another is by a meaningful silence that gives time for thought.

If you read your talk you will probably speak too quickly and either finish too soon or say more than your audience can cope with in the time available. Using cue cards and allocating time to each stage of your talk will make you realise how little you can say in the time available. For example, in a twenty-minute talk you may need three minutes for your introduction, three minutes for each of three main points, and three for your conclusion – leaving five minutes for questions. Nobody will mind if your talk finishes early, but you must not talk for too long.

Visual aids

Using a blackboard, white board or flip chart. Blackboards are more often misused than properly used. Perhaps this is why some people speak disparagingly of talk and chalk. However, used properly, a blackboard or a white board is an effective and versatile aid to quick and easy communication – and writing or drawing provides a change of medium for the audience and helps to prevent a speaker from presenting more information than an audience can cope with in the time available. A flip chart is similar but provides less space.

When using a blackboard, white board or flip chart remember the following points.

1 Yellow or white show up best against a dark green or black background, and black or dark blue against a white background.
2 Everyone is further away from the board than you are, so write in large clear block capitals.
3 Use diagrams that can be built up in stages, so that you can leave space at each stage for things that are to be added later.
4 When you are writing or drawing – stop talking. Try not to obscure anyone's view. Look at your audience whenever you are speaking to make sure you have their attention or that they are looking at what you want them to see.
5 People may need time to study any diagram without the distracting effect of your voice.
6 Remove any diagram as soon as you are ready to go on to the next stage in your talk. Do not allow people to look at one thing while you are trying to interest them in something else.

Using slides or overhead projector transparencies. In planning your talk decide when to show any slides. If you are actually using slides (not images stored electronically in a computer), it is disturbing to everyone if the lights are switched off and on repeatedly; and if the lights are off all the time you cannot see either your notes or the reactions of your audience to your message.

Even if the lights are on all the time, there are advantages of using any visual aids in one batch. For example, you could talk first and then use your visual aids to reinforce your main points before you state your conclusions; or you could use the visual aids to provide a break about half way through a longer talk.

Many speakers prefer to use slides or overhead transparencies, rather than a board or flip chart, for tables and diagrams. This saves time but a common result is that they say too much and show too many tables or diagrams in an attempt to present more information than people can assimilate in the time available.

When using slides or transparencies remember the following points.

1 Do not use too many visual aids.
2 Sit at the back of the room to check that the words, numbers and lines on each visual aid will be seen by your audience.

3 Use one visual aid to convey one message, and make that message brief, clear and simple so that it can be understood quickly.

4 Arrange the visual aids in the same order as your notes.

5 If you are actually using a slide projector, not images stored electronically in a computer, ensure that each slide is the right way up and the right way round.

6 Give people time to look at each visual aid before you add any explanation.

7 If you write on a transparency during your talk, for example to spell any word that might be new to some people in your audience, make sure the lines are distinct and the words legible.

8 Stand away from the screen. Use a pointer if you need to point at the screen.

9 Look at your audience, not at the screen, whenever you are speaking.

Giving your talk

If you are not used to speaking to an audience and feel apprehensive, your preparations and your concise notes or cue cards should reassure you that you are well prepared. Speak up but otherwise speak as you would to a small group of friends. That is to say, speak no faster than you would in normal conversation; and pause after each main point and to give people time to look at any visual aid.

Look at your audience to make sure you have their attention. Let them see your expressions and that you are interested in what you are saying and in their reactions to your message.

10

Working on a special study

A special study, involving an investigation or survey and a project report, or the preparation of a dissertation, extended essay or term paper, may be a major part of your final year's work – with the marks awarded affecting your final grade (for example see Table 10.1).

Table 10.1 Contribution of marks for special study, and marks for other course units, to the final mark upon which a student's grade is based

	Course units					
	1	2	3	4	5 (Special study)	Final mark
Student V	41	53	41	45	68	50
Student W	65	61	52	66	80	65
Student X	41	44	46	52	55	48
Student Y	46	44	56	48	52	49
Student Z	39	57	57	53	42	50

Because the special study provides opportunities for challenging, interesting and independent work, and to score marks outside the examinations, do not make the common mistake of devoting too much time to it. If you do, you may obtain a good mark for the special study but at the expense of poorer marks for other work (see marks of student V in Table 10.1). You are therefore advised to relate the amount of time you devote to the special study to its importance, in relation to other course units. For example, if one fifth of the marks available in the final year comes from each course unit and one fifth from the special study (see Table 10.1), you should allocate about one-fifth of your study time to each of these aspects of your work.

DECIDING WHAT TO STUDY

Agree the title and scope of the work proposed with your supervisor. You will need your supervisor's advice about what you can be expected to accomplish in the time available (see Table 10.2). Also, look at satisfactory compositions completed by other students in previous years of your course, to get an idea of what they were able to accomplish – but do not be impressed by their length and make sure that you do not exceed the number of words required.

Choose a subject in which you are already interested and which will complement and support your other studies. Either you or your supervisor should write concise *terms of reference* which state, as precisely as is possible at this stage, what you are required to do. These may have to be modified later, in the light of experience, with your supervisor's agreement. They should be neither too wide (so that all relevant sources of information could not be consulted in the time available) nor too narrow (dealing with a subject about which little has been published). Apart from the collection of material for inclusion, a major composition is required, which will probably be longer than any you have previously undertaken.

It is best to restrict any investigation to a particular aspect of the subject that will interest not only you but also your readers. However, it is probably best to avoid aspects about which you feel so strongly that you would find it difficult to produce a balanced composition.

Establish, at the outset, that any essential publications, equipment or materials will be available when you need them and for as long as you may need them.

HOW YOUR WORK WILL BE ASSESSED

All students taking a particular course will undertake special studies on different aspects of their subject – in contrast to most other course work in which all students answer the same question. In these extended exercises the students use different methods and have different supervisors, and differ in both their need for advice and in the amount of help they receive. All these differences must be considered by supervisors and examiners if each student's work is to be fairly assessed.

Clearly, you need to know how your composition is to be presented and how the work as a whole will be assessed. Marks are likely to be given for the way you approach and plan the work; for the thoroughness with which you gather and analyse data, and interpret the results; for initiative and originality; for your ability to relate your findings to the work of others; and for your ability to select relevant material and present this in a clear, concise and well organised dissertation, extended essay, term paper or project report.

YOUR COMPOSITION IS ALL THAT SOME ASSESSORS WILL SEE

Figure 10.1 A common mistake is to attempt too much, and to neglect other work.

Your composition should therefore indicate, as appropriate, not only what you have done but also your approach to the problems involved, to the critical evaluation of work done by others, and to the analysis and interpretation of any new observations. Because of all these things, as in all other assessed work, what you write and how well you write will play a major part in the assessment of your work. Remember that, apart from your supervisor, unless there is an oral examination, your composition is the assessor's only guide to the quality of your work (Fig. 10.1).

WORKING ON YOUR OWN

In a special study you work on your own but with your supervisor's advice when you need it (Table 10.2). You will have to gather information and organise your material before writing the essay or report. You may also collect original data – by observation alone, by observation and experiment, by interview or other survey methods, or by correspondence.

Table 10.2 Working, with supervision, on a special study

Activities	
Choosing a title Writing terms of reference	With supervisor.
Finding information Gathering data	Ask supervisor for advice when necessary.
Selecting Analysing Ordering Interpreting Summarising	Keep supervisor informed of progress.
Drafting report	Let supervisor see draft.
Revising report	Consider any comments.
Rewriting report	

Keep your supervisor informed of the way your work is going, but look upon the special study as an opportunity to work effectively on your own, to gather information from different sources, to assess its value in relation to your work, to show your knowledge of the subject, to organise and communicate the results of your thinking, and to complete the work on time.

REPORTING YOUR WORK

The students taking a particular course are likely to be given written instructions or notes for guidance. These are intended: (a) to help students with their writing, (b) to encourage uniformity, (c) to make for easy reading, and so (d) to facilitate marking.

These notes will indicate a maximum number of words to be used, when the composition is to be submitted for assessment, and how the work is to be presented (see Table 8.2, page 125).

A composition based on reading, with no supporting personal observations, will be written as a dissertation, extended essay, term paper, or review. As in any other essay, you will include an introduction and conclusion but the body of your essay will comprise many paragraphs. These must be arranged in an appropriate order, and you will help yourself and your readers if you group closely related paragraphs below appropriate headings and subheadings. You must therefore plan your work. This is even more important than in a shorter composition.

If a project involves the collection and analysis of data, as well as the study of relevant published work, the project report may be arranged as in Table 10.3. Using the accepted headings, and knowing the kind of information placed by convention below each heading, makes writing easier and helps the readers to find answers to their questions: Who? When? Where? What? Why? How?

Another type of project, preparing an instruction manual, may be appropriate in some courses. This manual may be arranged as follows: Cover; Title page; Acknowledgements; List of contents; Description of equipment; Operating instructions; Maintenance instructions; Servicing instructions; Fault-finding and fault-correction. In preparing instructions, as in all except imaginative writing, the essential characteristics are explanation, clarity, simplicity, completeness, accuracy, and good order. Each step should be distinct, and preferably it should be numbered, so that you know that you have completed one step before you start the next.

In other courses, a suitable project might be the preparation of a guide to the organisation and work of an agency, institution, firm or service. Such a project report might be arranged as follows: Cover;

Table 10.3 The parts of a project report

Part	Content
Cover sheet	Full title. Your name. Course title. Name of institution. Date.
Title page	Full title. Your name.
Acknowledgements	Who helped? In what way did they help? Mention only your supervisor and anyone who helped materially with your work. Do not use flowery language. For a typed report it is not necessary to name the typist.
List of contents	List of headings and subheadings used in your composition, with page numbers. In a short work this list may not be necessary.
Introduction	Why did you do this work? What was the problem? State your terms of reference. State briefly how this study is related to the work of others. Refer to things that you expect all your readers to know and build on this foundation: proceed from the general (subject area) to the particular (one aspect), or from the whole to its parts. In this way, give your readers a framework upon which the information and ideas presented in your composition can be hung. If a *Literature review* is required, include this at the end of the *Introduction* after a subheading.
Materials and methods	What materials did you use? How did you carry out your investigation? The purpose of this section is not only to inform but also to enable a reader to repeat the work and obtain similar data.
Results	State your findings simply and clearly. You may include diagrams and tables in which the results of your analysis of data are presented.
Discussion	What do you make of your results? How do they relate to the work of others – especially those mentioned in your *Introduction*. Do not express opinions as if they were facts, and do not present other people's opinions as if they were your own.
Conclusions	List your conclusions, which should follow logically from the *Results* and *Discussion* sections. Are you able to answer any of the questions raised in your *Introduction*? *Recommendations* may be listed at the end of this section, below a subheading.
Summary	What are your main findings? Be sure to include anything original, any achievements, and anything

Table 10.3 *Continued*

Part	Content
	else you particularly want the examiners to know about. The summary may be placed after the *Conclusions*, as indicated here, or immediately before the *Introduction*.
List of references	In your *Introduction, Materials and methods*, and *Discussion* sections, cite only publications that you have consulted. And in your list of references, give full bibliographic details (see page 92), for every publication cited (see page 112) but for no others.
Appendices	Tables of data, summarised in your *Results* section, may be included in an *Appendix*. Other relevant material that would be out of place in the body of your report may be included in other appendices, if your supervisor agrees that this would be appropriate.

Title page; Acknowledgements; List of contents; Introduction (including the reasons for the existence of the agency, institution etc., and the purpose of the project report); Method of enquiry (including how you obtained the information presented in your report, and what problems you encountered); Results (of your enquiry); Conclusions; Summary; Sources of information; Appendices.

If you are familiar with appropriate learned journals you will know how authors usually present their work in your subject, and how sources of information or ideas are usually acknowledged (see also pages 92 and 112).

Planning your composition

Allocate time to thinking, to collecting information, and to planning, writing and revising your composition (see Table 10.4). Start early. Finish on time. Then concentrate on other aspects of your course.

Do not spend so much time on reading that you have insufficient time to collect any necessary original data; and do not spend so much time collecting data that you have insufficient time to write. Unlike other shorter compositions prepared as part of course work or in examination, this longer work will not be completed at one sitting. Instead, you should think of writing as an aid to observation, thinking and planning, and to write throughout the time available for the work (see Tables 10.4 and 10.5).

Table 10.4   Allocation of time to a special study (say 6 hours per week for 22 weeks) *

Weeks from start

1	2	3	4	5	6	7	8	9	10	11	vacation	12	13	14	15	16	17	18	19	20	21	22
l																						
l	l																					
l	l	l																				
l	l	l	l																			
l	l	l	l	l		l		l		l		l				l		l				

Literature searching/reading

1	2	3	4	5	6	7	8	9	10	11	vacation	12	13	14	15	16	17	18	19	20	21	22
						d						d										
	d	d	d	d	d	d	d	d				d	d	d								
	d	d	d	d	d	d	d	d				d	d	d		d						
	d	d	d	d	d	d	d	d				d	d	d	d	d	d	d				
	d	d	d	d	d	d	d	d				d	d	d	d	d	d	d				
	d	d	d	d	d	d	d	d				d	d	d	d	d	d	d				

Data collection

1	2	3	4	5	6	7	8	9	10	11	vacation	12	13	14	15	16	17	18	19	20	21	22
																			r	r	p	p
																			r	r	p	p
		w																w	r	r	p	p
	w	w							w	w	w		w	w	w	w	w	w	r	r	p	p
w	w	w			w		w		w	w	w	w	w	w	w	w	w	w	r	r	p	p

Writing   Revising and word processing

* *Note.* Each symbol represents about an hour's work.
l = literature search, d = data collection, w = writing, r = revising, p = word processing.

Plan your composition and select appropriate headings as soon as possible, so that you can select and file relevant material under these headings. At this stage, use your topic outline as your contents page.

If you have good keyboard skills, word processing can help you in all four stages of composition and help you to prepare a long composition more easily and quickly than would otherwise be possible (see Appendix B Computer appreciation, page 200). However, even if you have good keyboard skills there are advantages in working on a hand-written first draft. In particular, you can work on a hand-written composition wherever you are.

You are therefore advised to hand-write each paragraph on a separate sheet of A4 paper. Start with words from the topic sentence of the paragraph as a heading and add relevant notes below this heading. This will enable you to say all you need to say on each topic on one side of one sheet of paper, to change the order of paragraphs if necessary, and to add new paragraphs (concerned with additional topics) in the most appropriate places as your work proceeds – as you would if using a word processor.

When your composition is otherwise complete, you will probably delete the paragraph headings. They help you to ensure relevance and order but are unlikely to help the reader. Even in a long composition you should not need more than three levels of heading. These should be distinguished in a hierarchy. For example, section or chapter headings could be centred in capital letters, sub-subsection headings in capitals but not centred, and each heading within a sub-section in lower case except for a capital initial letter. Each of these headings should have a line to itself; and it is usual to start each section or chapter at the top of a page, to leave three lines blank before sub-section headings, to leave two lines blank after sub-section headings, and to leave one line blank between paragraphs, and before each heading within a sub-section.

Alternatively, in technical subjects, capital letters may be used for the initial letter only of each heading, with no headings centred and with a hierarchy indicated by decimal or point numbering (for example, 1 for the first section heading, 1.1 for the first sub-section heading within section 1, and 1.1.1 for the first sub-heading within sub-section 1.1).

Starting to write

Unless you are using a word processor for planning, writing and revising your composition, you are advised to keep a copy, using carbon paper (so that you can make copies anywhere, as you write), of each sheet in a different place from your top copies. If you do not do so, and you lose your only copy of your composition, you will have to start again from the beginning – if there is time – and at best this will interfere with your other work. If you are using a word processor, make sure that you always have an up-to-date copy of your composition on disk, in a safe place, in addition to the copy on which you are working (see page 203).

Start writing as soon as you have decided what to study. Writing a first draft of the *Introduction* will concentrate your attention on the purpose and scope of your composition and its relationship to the published work of others. This should help you to see your limited objective, clearly stated in your terms of reference, in a wider perspective.

In a dissertation, extended essay, or term paper, in any subject, your introduction may include a proposition: a statement offered for consideration, which will be followed in the rest of the work by argument, supported by evidence, and which in the last paragraph you may conclude is probably correct, or which you may reject, or you may have insufficient evidence to reach either conclusion.

In a project report, as part of an enquiry or investigation (for example, in business, engineering, market research or science), your *Introduction* must include a clear statement of the problem investigated – which may be written as a question. If an experiment is reported, the hypothesis tested – a possible answer to the question – should also be stated. The *Methods* section must be written at the beginning, as soon as you have decided on your procedures. Then data can be collected, recorded on data sheets, and analysed, and the results summarised for the *Results* section, as the work proceeds.

Notes can also be made, throughout the work, of points to be included in the *Discussion* section. In this way the parts of the first draft can be written in more or less the correct order.

You will also find it helpful to record the complete bibliographic details of each reference consulted during your literature survey and in your further or background reading, on a separate index card (see page 92).

If you work in this way, you will have regular practice in writing and your composition will be revised regularly so that it remains an up-to-date progress report that can be completed soon after other aspects of the work are finished. Another advantage of working in this way is that, if necessary, you can check your work while any equipment or sources of information needed for the work are still available and there is still time (see Table 10.4).

Reviewing the literature

The more specialised your work, or the more recent the published work you need to study, the less you will be able to rely on books and the more you will need to look at papers in journals that publish original work of specialists (see pages 101–2). You should also be aware of journals that publish review articles in your subject, of relevant conference proceedings, and of official reports. Most academic libraries provide concise guides to the literature in different subjects. You should also discuss sources of information with your supervisor.

In addition to the resources available in your own library and in other local libraries, you may be able to enter keywords (search terms) using a computer terminal with access to abstracting and indexing publications on CD-ROM or via the Internet to bibliographic databases in other institutions (see page 103). However, you should check that the resources you need are not readily available locally before spending time and money trying to obtain them from other sources.

When you have completed your literature search you may have bibliographic details of many relevant publications. You will then have to select, on the basis of their titles, or from abstracts, or from references in other publications, *and with your supervisor's advice*, those that are likely to be of most interest to you.

In reviewing the literature, read critically (see page 89). You will recognise *opinions* (views on the basis of evidence and experience but which are not necessarily correct), *assumptions* (things assumed to be true but which may not be), *assertions* (things stated as if they were true but for which no evidence is provided by the writer), *facts* (things which on the basis of all the evidence at present available are generally accepted as true statements) and *speculation* (which may or may not be well founded, and so could be helpful or misleading). You will draw attention to conflicting statements, and to *issues* (points of contention). You may make comparisons, recognise connections, suggest different interpretations, and come to your own conclusions or point to the need for further research.

Preparing diagrams and tables

If you include diagrams and tables, each one should be planned so that it fits upright on the page, and should occupy a separate sheet of paper unless you wish to facilitate comparison. There should be an appropriate legend (below each figure) or heading (above each table), as in this book. Diagrams and tables should be numbered, separately, so that you can refer to them in any part of your composition.

Make sure that you do refer to each diagram and to each table, at least once, in your composition. You should need fewer words in the text because information presented in a diagram or table should not be repeated in the text. Nor should information be presented in both a diagram and a table: convey your message clearly and once only.

Writing for your readers

Remember, in preparing any communication, that it is not enough to write something that *you* can understand. This is especially important when you are reporting on work in which you have been involved for some time. You should be closer to the investigation, and therefore more familiar with your material, than your readers. In starting to read, they are at the beginning of your investigation, whereas you are at the end.

All reports have both primary readers (those who asked for the report and who may make a decision or take action on the basis of the report) and secondary readers (who receive the report for information only and who read only the title and, perhaps, the *Introduction, Conclusions*, and *Summary*). Primary readers (who may know almost as much as you do about your project) may be expected to read the whole report and to understand every sentence. Secondary readers of a project report are those who are experts on other subjects but who are unlikely to be as well informed as your supervisor (or yourself) on the subject considered in your composition. Write for your primary readers in the first place, and then make sure that your *Introduction, Conclusions*, and *Summary*, at least, could be understood by a secondary reader.

In all parts of a report your meaning should be expressed as simply and clearly as possible, and technical terms should be either avoided if they might not be understood by some secondary readers or sufficiently explained when they are first used.

Consider your readers. Who are they? Your supervisor is closest to the work; the second internal assessor is unlikely to be a specialist in the same area of work; and you do not know the external assessor's interests.

Whenever you speak or write, try to express yourself not only in words that you understand but also in a way that will be understood by others. This is not an easy task, but you are unlikely to communicate effectively unless you consider the needs of your audience.

Preparing the typescript

Check your completed composition, on which your work will be assessed, using the check list in Table 10.5 as a guide, and make any changes you consider necessary. Check that you have used capital letters or underlined words (to be printed in italics or underlined (see page 125) only where necessary, and that the exact position of each table and each figure is clearly indicated, so that spaces can be left for them in the typescript.

When you are happy with the composition yourself, it is a good idea to ask someone who has not been closely connected with your work to read it to see if they can find any obvious mistakes, any unnecessary technical terms, or any sentences that are not clearly expressed. Then your supervisor may like to see your work before it is typed.

Consider any suggestions and, if necessary, revise your composition. Unless you word process it yourself, you will need to ensure that it is legible and neatly set out – with any instructions about arrangement and presentation stated clearly. If you cannot obtain precise instructions as to how your work is to be set out, you may find it helpful to look at similar compositions prepared by other students in previous years. If no precise guidance is available, in your course guide or from your supervisor, the following instructions should enable you (or anyone with experience of this kind of work) to produce an acceptable typescript.

1 Print on good quality A4 paper, and keep one copy on disk in a safe place (separate from the one on which you are working).
2 Leave a 40 mm margin on the left and a 25 mm margin on the right, top and bottom of each page.
3 Use a standard typeface (for example Times Roman), 12 point print size, and type double spacing on one side of each sheet only.
4 Centre each main heading, in upper case, at the top of a new page.
5 Do not justify right hand margins.
6 Do not centre sub-headings, but give them a line to themselves. Use upper case (capital letters).
7 Use a capital initial letter for the first word of any headings in each sub-section, and give each of these headings a line to itself.
8 Leave one space after a comma or semi-colon, after each initial in a person's name, and between a number and a symbol for an SI unit of measurement. Leave two spaces after a full stop and in main headings between words printed in capitals. Do not put a

full stop after a heading if it has a line to itself. Do not put a full stop after an SI unit unless it is at the end of a sentence.

9 Do not underline headings. Underline only those words that in a book would be printed in italics – or print them in italics (see Table 8.2, page 125).

10 Leave three lines blank after a section or chapter heading and before a sub-heading, two lines blank after a sub-heading, and one line blank after a sub-heading and between paragraphs.

11 Type each table on a separate sheet, with a heading immediately after the table number, at the top of the page.

12 Include separate cover and title pages; and a list of contents.

13 When the tables and figures have been inserted, number all pages, except the cover, title and contents pages.

Keep a copy for your records.

Table 10.5 Checking a dissertation, extended essay, term paper or project report

1 Have you followed any instructions or notes for guidance provided as part of your course?

2 Are the cover and title pages complete (see Table 10.3)?

3 Does the title still provide the best concise description of the contents of your composition?

4 Is the *List of Contents* necessary? Check, if it is, that all the headings and sub-headings are arranged in the same order and worded as in the text.

5 Does each part of the composition start with a main heading at the top of a new page?

6 Is everything in the composition relevant to the title and to the preceding heading?

7 Have you kept to the terms of reference agreed with your supervisor and are these clearly stated in the *Introduction*?

8 Is any information presented in a table repeated in a diagram or, unnecessarily, in the text?

9 Are any tables and diagrams correctly numbered, on separate sheets, and referred to in appropriate places in the text?

10 Is each statement accurate, based on sufficient evidence, free from contradictions, and free from errors of omission?

11 Are all sources cited in your composition listed separately at the end, and in alphabetical order, in a bibliography or list of references (see page 113)

12 Is anything original in your composition emphasised sufficiently?

13 Are your conclusions clearly expressed?

14 Check all other aspects of your work, as you would on completing a shorter composition (see page 124 and Table 8.2). Then, if necessary, revise your work.

Part 3

Revision and examination techniques

Most of the time, in study, you will be occupied with current work or looking forward to what you are about to do next, but you should also allocate some study periods every week, particularly at week-ends and in vacations, to revision (see pages 26 and 34).

Revision (looking again) starts soon after each lecture, preferably on the same evening, when you check your notes (see page 59). Even if you are not consciously trying to remember, thinking again will help you to understand and will help to stop you forgetting! Similarly, each private study period should end with a quick review of your work in that period and with revision (see, for example, page 40). Psychologists call such revision of things that you already know, in regular short periods throughout your course, over-learning. It is a method of fixing things in your mind.

By using effective study techniques, completing all assessed course work set, and revising regularly, you should be well prepared for your tests and examinations. However, even if you have not attended organised classes regularly and do not have good notes, or have not revised regularly, you can reduce anxiety before an examination and improve your marks in the examination by looking at recent examination papers, preparing topic outlines to possible questions, and preparing other concise revision notes (as recommended in Chapter 11) and by improving your examination techniques (as recommended in Chapter 12).

11

Preparing for examinations

CONSIDER WHAT IS EXPECTED OF YOU

Your performance in tests and examinations, and perhaps also in assessed course work (see pages 124 and 127) determines your progress through the course and your final result. Your purpose in study, therefore, will be not only to master your subjects but also to do as well as possible in all assessed work.

One of the main causes of under-achievement is the student's failure to understand just what is required in a particular course. Apart from good organisation, a sustained and well directed effort is required. An understanding of what is expected in your course is obtained from: (a) your lecture notes, which with the course guide indicate the scope of the work upon which you will be examined, (b) your textbooks and other recommended reading; (c) the questions set in previous years' examination papers, (d) the exercises set in class and for homework, and (e) the comments written on your assessed course work.

In assessed course work, always try to learn from any comments or corrections and try to read the work of other students who scored higher marks. This will help you to see not only where you went wrong but also how other people have conveyed information and ideas – perhaps more completely or more effectively than you did.

If, after looking through your own work (and that of other students), you still do not see where you went wrong, or if you do not understand any comments or corrections written on your work, make a point of asking the assessor for advice or help, just as you would ask a lecturer for help if you did not understand any point made in a lecture.

For many courses, students are given a course guide when they arrive at college. This may include a list of the names of academic staff, a course outline, a syllabus or list of learning outcomes, a reading list, and information about course work including homework, examinations, and assessment. Alternatively, information may be available in the college library, or may be displayed on notice boards, or individual lecturers may introduce themselves and outline what they will be teaching. Ask the Departmental Secretary, the lecturer concerned, or your personal tutor, if you do not have all the information you require. You need information on all these aspects of your work at the beginning of the course.

Also find out if there are any committees (e.g. course committees and staff-student liaison committees) on which students are represented. Talk to your elected representatives on such committees if there is any matter relating to the course that you consider should be discussed.

Always do homework, even if the marks given will not contribute to the grade awarded at the end of your course (see page 127). Undertaking set work, regularly, provides valuable practice. The marks given indicate the value of each piece of work and are a guide to your progress. And any comments or corrections, if considered carefully, should help you to do better work next time. In this way your final grade will be affected indirectly, even if the marks scored in course work do not contribute directly, because you will be able to complete better answers in your final examinations.

Good study techniques, as recommended in this book, are an aid to effective study. However, flexibility is needed. Different techniques will be used on different occasions. Different subjects, different lecture courses, different lecturers, and different methods of assessment, all make different demands – and an intelligent student should be able to respond in different ways.

USE APPROPRIATE TEXTBOOKS

Some students use school textbooks as a basis for more advanced studies at college. This is usually a mistake. Your lecture notes should provide a foundation, and you should build on this by making regular and frequent use of the textbooks recommended for your present course. For further information and for background reading, get into the habit of looking at more than one source to get different opinions and approaches.

Some students consult out-of-date textbooks and reference books. However, remember that you cannot expect to obtain an up-to-date account of a subject from a book written many years ago. Always look at the date of publication and try to obtain the most recent edition of each book you consult (see page 86).

LOOK AT SYLLABUSES AND COURSE GUIDES

Before applying for a course you should have seen an outline of the whole course, so that you know what choice of subjects, if any, is available. Then, at the start of each year, look at the course guide or at the year guide. This will give a good indication of what you will be studying during the year, as well as indicating the scope of the examinations, and will help you to see the course in perspective, week by week.

It is a good idea to copy each part of the syllabus (details of course content) or list of learning outcomes (things you should know, understand or be able to do after completing the course) on a separate sheet of paper and to file this at the start of your notes on each aspect of the subject. Remember, however, that your best and only complete guide to the course content should be your record, in your own notes, made in lectures, tutorials, and other classes, throughout the course.

The syllabus and your lecture notes provide a foundation for your further studies (see page 57). They should set limits to your studies, so that you are not easily side-tracked into some aspects whilst others are neglected, but these limits should not be so rigid as to discourage independent thought and enquiry.

LOOK AT RECENT EXAMINATION PAPERS

Obtain copies of the examination papers for the last two years, taken by students who followed the same course. Two years' question papers will usually be enough. If you go too far back you may waste time looking at papers set when the syllabus was different and set by different examiners.

Look to see which aspects of the subject are examined on each examination paper; and if any papers are divided into parts note which aspects are examined in each part.

Past question papers are your only guide to the *arrangement* of *questions* on the paper and to the *kind of choice* of question that has to be made. The instructions at the head of the paper may state, for example, that you must answer question one and three others, or that you must answer at least one question from each section. You may also be advised to devote a certain proportion of your time to one particular question, or to one part of the paper.

Similarly, recent question papers are a guide to the *kinds of questions* that are likely to be set. You may find that there is always one question with many parts, each requiring a short answer. Another question may provide much of the information you need for a complete answer: if you read it carefully before preparing your answer. Some questions may be structured, indicating clearly the parts of your answer (for example, by letters or by the subheadings to be used). Others may require essay-type answers. If particular kinds of question have been set for the last two years, you may expect a similar balance of questions in your examinations.

PLAN ANSWERS TO EXAMINATION QUESTIONS

It is a good idea to copy each question, from the last two years' examination papers, at the top of a separate sheet of notepaper, leaving space for a plan of your answer. Then file each question with your revision notes on the subject.

Planning answers to examination questions helps you to recall what you know and to reorganise your thoughts in the form of an answer to the question asked. It will help you to think, to recognise gaps in your knowledge or understanding, and to learn, and so is part of active study. Try to work things out for yourself, first, but discuss any question with a lecturer if you are not sure of its precise meaning, or if you are not sure what is required in the answer, or if you think that your plan may be incomplete or otherwise incorrect.

Planning answers to the kinds of questions that are likely to be set in your examinations is good practice. You are also advised to write out some answers in full.

In some weeks throughout the course your set work will involve answering questions similar to those set in examinations. In other weeks set yourself questions. There is no better preparation for examinations than completing answers to suitable questions in the amount of time that would be available in an examination – even if you devote more time to thinking about and planning your answer.

If there is to be a change in the kinds of questions set, the arrangement of questions on the paper, the kinds of choice to be made, or the aspects of the subject to be examined on each paper, then candidates should be told about the change well before the examinations. They should be given examples of the new kinds of questions, or specimen examination papers to illustrate the new format.

PREPARE REVISION AIDS FROM YOUR NOTES

Notes made when you are thinking or reading should be combined with your lecture notes on the same subject – so that you have only one set of notes (see Figure 7.2, page 96).

Nevertheless, you are likely to find as the course of study proceeds that your notes are becoming too bulky. Your notes, for all the subjects you are taking in examinations, will probably be too long to read in the few weeks preceding examinations. They may be suitable for reference but not for revision.

In earlier revision periods, therefore, throughout the course, you are advised to make shorter revision notes, from your notes, on each aspect of your work (Figure 11.1). These concentrated revision notes should be, for examples: (a) lists of basic ideas, (b) concise summaries, (c) topic outlines, (d) annotated diagrams, and (e) definitions that you must remember.

Each list, summary, outline, diagram or definition, should be on one side of a sheet of paper or, preferably, on one side of an index card (or postcard) for quick reference and for rapid but frequent

MAKE SHORT REVISION NOTES - PERHAPS ON INDEX CARDS

Figure 11.1 Your notes will probably be so long that you could not read them in the last few weeks before an examination.

reading. File these cards, in a card index, but always have a few in your pocket and study them on bus and train journeys, while you are waiting for appointments, and whenever you have a few moments to spare for private study. These cards will be invaluable in the weeks before examinations when you must revise each subject as a whole.

Annotated diagrams make very good revision aids – helping you, for example, to visualise a pattern or sequence of events. Include diagrams in your notes as aids to learning and revision: visualising the whole will help you to recall the parts. Also, if appropriate, prepare simpler diagrams that could be reproduced quickly and neatly if you decided to include them in an examination answer (see Figures 11.2 and 11.3) to convey information, reduce the number of words needed in a description or explanation, and save time.

Preparing revision aids, because it makes you think again about each aspect of your work and concentrate on essentials, is in itself an effective revision technique. Having prepared a revision note on any subject you will find that you have fixed many things that you wished to learn in your mind.

You look, think, select, arrange, and write or draw – and this active study aids concentration. In preparing concise summaries of

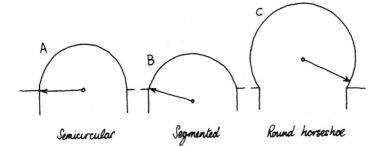

Figure 11.2 Simple diagrams, drawn quickly, to illustrate three different types of arches used by architects.

your earlier work you see connections with your later work, and this increases your understanding. You also learn by reorganising your early work in the light of your further experience – of the subject, of making notes, and of the kinds of records that you require.

TEST YOURSELF

If you sit reading notes, just trying to remember them, you may find concentration difficult and may remember very little. Furthermore, memorising is not enough: most questions test both your knowledge and your understanding. Throughout your course, therefore, it is best to devote revision periods – like other study periods – to different kinds of activity. Consider what you need to know about each aspect of your work. Then set yourself definite tasks.

1 *Set* yourself questions of different kinds, that could be set in your examinations: analyse, define, explain etc. (see page 136).
2 *Solve* any problems, from your textbooks, that you have not tackled previously.
3 *Organise* your knowledge of a subject – as you would before giving a lecture to next year's students taking the same course.
4 *Make* notes of any gaps in your knowledge and then, at the next opportunity, try to fill these gaps.
5 *Prepare* a topic outline for a question set earlier in the course, then compare this with the answer you wrote at the time. Could you write a better answer now?
6 *Prepare* simple diagrams from memory and then compare these with similar diagrams prepared previously.

ROCK FORMATIONS

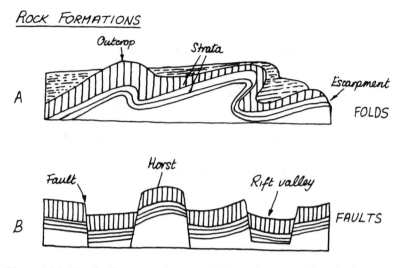

Figure 11.3 Simple diagrams, drawn quickly and annotated to facilitate the definition of terms used in describing geological features.

7 *Recall* the main points on one aspect of a subject. Make notes and then compare them with your concentrated revision notes.
8 *Read* your revision notes repeatedly, especially in the last weeks preceding an examination.
9 *Write* definitions, from memory, then check these against your revision notes or textbook.

PLAN YOUR REVISION

Revision is not something that can be left until the last few weeks immediately before an examination. It is part of active study.

Throughout your course, each time you look again at past work, you not only think about each topic again but also see it in the light of your further experience of the subject as a whole. As you work on your notes (see pages 58 and 95) you think again about a subject and understand it better. Furthermore, between periods of revision, you think about your subjects, assimilate information, and see connections between different aspects of your work. In this way you learn many things without the conscious effort of trying to remember them.

Regular revision (see Table 5.1, page 69) helps you to understand past work, to cope better with current work, and to approach examinations with confidence.

The weeks before an examination

For your final revision you will probably devote more time than usual to study: perhaps working 56 hours each week instead of 49 hours (see page 28). But continue to allocate enough time to recreation and sleep in the weeks preceding your examinations. After even a short period of recreation you will feel refreshed and ready to return to active study; and a good night's sleep will help you to avoid undue anxiety and to concentrate on your work.

Remember that in revision you should be looking at things again in the light of the course as a whole. You should be checking for accuracy and completeness, concentrating on essentials, and refreshing your memory. *You should not be learning things for the first time.* Do not miss organised classes towards the end of your course in order to spend the time on revision. These last classes may prove to be most useful. The lecturer may emphasise important points, draw conclusions, and sum up at the end of the course.

If your study time has been well organised, so that your thoughts are well organised, you will have a good set of revision notes. Your final revision will be much easier and much more effective than would otherwise be possible.

Start your final revision in good time – say eight weeks before the first examination (Table 11.1). Work to a timetable so that you are in control and you do not waste time at the start of each study session, deciding what to do. Revise each subject over the whole revision period. Do not revise one subject at a time: if you do you may run out of time and fail to revise some aspects of your work.

Make a note of the times and locations of all your examinations in your diary, as soon as the examinations' timetable is available.

In looking at past examination papers you may see that questions are set nearly every year on certain topics. Also, from the emphasis placed on certain aspects of your work (the amount of time devoted to them in organised classes) you may think that questions are likely to be set on these aspects. Most students try to guess which questions are likely to be included in their examinations. However, it is

Table 11.1 Example of a plan of work for the eight weeks preceding an examination*

Weeks	Activities
8	Survey the course as a whole, as indicated by the course guide and your notes made in class. Look at examination papers for the last two years. Consider which aspects require most attention in your revision.
7–6	Look through all your notes, checking that you have a complete set of revision notes.
5–4	Memorize revision notes. Write out revision notes from memory.
3	Prepare topic outlines and write complete answers to some questions. Memorise revision notes.
2	Set yourself a test paper, including questions you think may be set in your examination. Answer this in the time that will be allowed in your examination, then compare your answers with topic outlines prepared previously. Assess your own work. Read selected passages, on which you think you are likely to be examined, from textbooks. Memorise your revision notes.
1	Set yourself another test paper. Assess your work. Look through all your revision notes again to refresh your memory.

*Prepare your own revision plan to suit your needs.

best to master each subject and to revise all aspects of your work so that it does not matter too much if some of your favourite topics are not examined. In taking examinations you should not be taking chances.

There are other dangers in trying to spot questions (guessing which questions are likely to be set). Some students prepare answers to these questions so that they can let the words flow forth in the examination, like a dam bursting. This is a complete waste of time if the question is not on the examination paper. And it is almost a complete waste of time if the question set is not quite the same as expected – so that a different answer is needed. The prepared answer will not do.

It is best to prepare topic outlines for the different kinds of questions that you are likely to be asked, so that in the examination you can consider the actual question set and then prepare an appropriate topic outline immediately before you start to write.

Questions may be set on all the things that you have been taught. And you will be expected, especially in advanced courses, to demonstrate by citing sources in your answers (see page 112) that you have studied the subject yourself. As a result of observing, reading, and thinking, you should know more than you have been taught.

12

Taking tests and examinations

The best way to avoid anxiety about coursework, tests and examinations, and to ensure that you obtain grades that are a true reflection of your ability, is to have a positive attitude to your work (see page 12). Having studied and revised subjects in which you are interested, you should be well prepared.

The use of effective study and revision techniques should help you, as your knowledge and understanding increase, to approach tests and examinations with confidence. Each one is a challenge that provides opportunities: (a) for you to display your knowledge, reasoning ability and understanding; and (b) for your progress to be assessed.

TAKING TESTS AS PART OF COURSE WORK

Tests differ from examinations in that they comprise questions that require only short answers. They are useful as part of course work because they can test your knowledge and understanding of most topics included in the syllabus or list of learning objectives for the course. Regular tests serve to remind students that revision is part of active study, and help them to recognise gaps in their knowledge or understanding – and then rectify any weaknesses. Test results also provide feedback to assessors – indicating parts of the course that some students are finding difficult, and helping them to identify particular students who need extra tutorial instruction or guidance.

In some courses tests are used not only to promote learning and to improve teaching but also to provide marks that contribute to the final assessment of each student's performance. This is fair to all students, in that they are all assessed at the same time, answering identical questions, under examination conditions. But, like assessments based on homework, if such tests are held during the course they have the disadvantage that students are being tested while they are still learning – before they have had the opportunity to benefit from the course as a whole (see page 126). That is to say, an attempt is being made to assess learning outcomes before it is possible to know the outcomes, and in this sense such tests are contrary to the whole spirit of higher education and the encouragement of personal development. If to avoid this the tests are held only at the end of the course they are useful as a method of assessment – and they are easier to mark than examinations in which essay-type answers are required – but they do not contribute to effective teaching and learning in the ways indicated on page 129.

Answering questions in tests

Prepare for each test as you would for an examination, but use a different technique when taking a test: (a) if each question requires only a short answer, and (b) if you are required to answer every question.

Because only short answers are required, and you may be tested on all aspects of the course, if you have missed even one class you may be unable to answer some questions.

Because you have to answer all the questions, it would be a waste of time to read all the questions first – as you would if you had to decide which ones to answer and in what order to answer them.

Instead, read the first question. Think about it. If you are sure you understand exactly what is required, and you know the answer, write your answer at once. There may be space on the question paper for your answer. If there is, accept this as an indication of the length of answer expected. Do not try to write more. The number of marks available for a complete and correct answer to the question may also be stated. If it is, this may be an indication of the number of different points you are expected to make in your answer. As you complete your answer, put a tick in the left hand margin of the page next to the question number.

Work through the paper answering all the questions you know you can answer correctly, but not spending time thinking about any question if the answer does not come immediately to mind. Instead of a tick, put a question mark in the margin of the test paper, next to the question number, to remind you to look again at this question if you have time.

In this way you will ensure that you do answer all the questions you feel confident you can answer correctly, whereas if you were to spend too long thinking and worrying about any questions you found difficult you could run out of time and find that you had not answered some easy questions.

If you have time, after working through the paper once, go through the paper again tackling the questions you did not answer the first time through. You may find, on second thoughts, that you can answer some of them.

If you do not know the answer to any question, and you know that you will not lose marks for an incorrect answer, you must guess. Just by chance some of your guesses are likely to be correct – and score some marks. In a multiple choice test, choose the answer you think is most likely to be correct. From your knowledge of the subject you can make guesses that are more likely to be right than wrong.

TAKING EXAMINATIONS

If you have revised regularly throughout your course (see page 170) you should be keyed-up and ready for action – as an athlete would be, after months of training, immediately before a race. You should not be over-anxious. However, the advice in this chapter should help all students to approach examinations with greater confidence.

As a student you should have a desire to learn, but examinations are an additional incentive. Each examination passed provides encouragement and satisfaction, confirming that you have reached a certain standard. However, many students do not do as well as they could in examinations. Sometimes this is because they have not worked hard enough and *do not know as much about their subjects as they should*. Sometimes it is because, although they have worked hard, they have not organised their study time effectively; and sometimes they have worked hard, organised their studies, know their subjects, and yet have not thought enough about examination technique.

Learn from other students' mistakes

(a) Master your subjects

The most common reason for failure in examinations is inadequate preparation. To master all subjects, you need to develop your interest in them (see Chapter 1); keep fit for study (Chapter 2); use your time effectively and concentrate during hours of study (Chapter 3); study effectively (Chapters 4 to 8); develop your ability to use language effectively (Chapter 9); and revise your work regularly throughout the course (Chapter 11).

(b) Select questions as directed in the instructions at the head of the question paper

Some candidates fail to answer compulsory questions – and can therefore score no marks for them. They cannot make good this omission by answering extra questions from other parts of the paper. Such extra questions will not be marked.

Some candidates when asked, for example, to answer four questions and to answer at least one from each of the sections of the paper A, B and C, answer no questions from one section. They can score no marks, therefore, for this section. And the examiner will mark only three questions from the other sections, even if four have been answered.

(c) Select questions carefully

Some candidates do not read the whole paper before deciding which questions to answer.

If an examination paper comprises many questions, each requiring only a short answer, and if all questions are to be answered, then it is probably best to start at the beginning and to work through to the end – as in a test. Each question can be read, understood, considered, and a short answer recorded. Any question that is not answered immediately can be reconsidered later.

However, most advanced examinations are not of this kind. If there is a choice, you must allow a proportion of the time available for reading all the questions carefully. Consider what is required in each answer before deciding which you can answer best. If you do not do this, you may find, after completing the examination, that you could have made a better choice and scored higher marks.

(d) Answer the required number of questions

Some candidates do not answer the required number of questions. The marks allocated to each question may be indicated on the examination paper. Otherwise, the same number of marks will be available for each question. For example, if four questions have to be answered this means that up to twenty-five marks could be scored for each question. If a student attempts five questions, only the first four answers will be marked: no marks will be given for the fifth answer. To answer more than the required number of questions is a waste of time – and it reduces the time you can devote to answers that will be marked. On the other hand, students who answer only three or two questions, when they should answer four, will be marked out of seventy-five and fifty, respectively.

You must do your best to answer the right number of questions. However, if you find that you are unable to do this, do your best to cope with the situation: *keep your head*. If you should answer four questions but can answer only three, work steadily at these three questions and you may still score high marks. And if you can answer only two you may still pass the examination. You should also be able to score some marks by giving incomplete answers to some questions. If necessary, do this to make up the number of answers required.

(e) Allocate your time according to the marks available

Some candidates spend too much time on some questions, so that they cannot spend enough on others. They may even find that they have no time for their last answer. Make sure that you know how much time is allowed for the whole examination: then divide your time wisely. The instructions at the head of the paper may include advice about how much time should be spent on each part of the paper.

If the marks available for a question (or for the parts of a question) are stated on the paper, next to the question, this also indicates how you should allocate your time.

If the questions carry equal marks try to allocate your time equally between them (see Table 12.1). Resist the temptation to spend more time on those questions that you feel you can answer best (see Table 12.2). Remember that it is easier to score a few marks on a question that you at first felt you did not know much about than to score a few extra marks by spending extra time on what is already a good answer.

If you spend fifty minutes on a question that should be answered in thirty-six, you are probably including irrelevant material, or padding; or saying the same thing twice (perhaps using different

Table 12.1 Allocating your time in an examination

Time allowed for examination	Number of questions to be answered	Available for each question	
		Time*	Marks
180 min	6	30 min	16.7
	5	36 min	20
	4	45 min	25
	3	60 min	33.3

* Deduct from the time available for each question, the time needed for reading all the questions, deciding which questions to answer, and checking your answers.

Table 12.2 Three ways of allocating your time in a three-hour written examination, and the possible consequences

Question	Time allocation	Marks	Time allocation	Marks	Time allocation	Marks
1	55 min	16*	55 min	16*	36 min	14
2	50 min	14	50 min	14	36 min	13
3	40 min	11	40 min	11	36 min	12
4	35 min	11	20 min	8	36 min	11
5		0	15 min	6	36 min	10*
Totals		52		55		60

* In a written answer it is difficult to score more than sixteen out of twenty for a good answer, and it is relatively easy to score half marks by attending carefully to a question that you at first thought you did not know much about.

words); or giving unnecessary detail, extra examples, or more explanation than is necessary.

If you do find that you are running out of time, towards the end of an examination, it is better to write a good topic outline for a complete answer or to answer the question in note-form, than to leave a question unanswered or to write only the first parts of an answer that you do not have time to complete.

(f) Answer precisely the question asked not a slightly different question that you expected

Some candidates, during their revision, prepare an answer to a question set in a previous year that they think may be set again this year. Then they write their prepared answer in the examination – even though the question set is not identical with the one they expected. That is to say, they fail to respond to the exact wording of the question (see page 136). The result, at best, is that they cannot score full marks. At worst, they may write at length, including some things that would have been relevant if they had been presented as an answer to the question asked, and yet score no marks.

If you plan an answer during your revision, do read the question set in the examination carefully, to make sure that you do know exactly what is required. Plan your answer to the question set: then include only relevant material in *your answer to this question*.

(g) Keep to the point

Some students, because they do not know the answer to the question set or do not read the question carefully, write more than is required and yet still do not answer the question. Perhaps remembering a relevant lecture, or having memorised several pages of notes on the subject, they insist on pouring forth all that they know. Instead they should be giving a considered answer: selecting and arranging only relevant points from their notes – and adding relevant information and ideas from other sources.

If asked to give a reasoned account of the circumstances leading to an event, a student might mention some things that happened before the event, describe the event in detail, and then discuss some after-effects. Yet there could be no marks for the description of the event, nor for discussing its after-effects, because the question did not ask for these things. And because only some circumstances leading to the event are mentioned, this part of the composition could not be considered well reasoned or complete. In other words, much time might be spent on this work and the student might feel pleased at having remembered so much and at covering so many pages with writing – yet very few marks could be awarded.

(h) Answer all parts of the question

When examinations are set the examiners prepare outlines of the answers they expect. Then they allocate marks to the parts of each answer or for each of the topics expected in a complete answer. You are likely to score most marks if, before starting to write, you prepare a plan that includes all the topics in the examiner's marking scheme (preferably in the same order). This is why you must read the question carefully and then think about what should be included in a complete and balanced answer. If some parts of the question are not answered you cannot score the marks available for these parts.

In structured questions, which indicate clearly the separate parts required in an answer, consider what is required in each part. Also, use your judgement in deciding how many marks are likely to be available for each part. Then allocate your time accordingly. If you spend too much time on one aspect of your answer you cannot score more than the number of marks allocated for this part. If you then spend too little time on other aspects you may not make the best use of your knowledge and so you are likely to score fewer marks than you should. For any aspects that you ignore, you can score no marks. You must appreciate the need to plan each answer, so that you can visualise the probable marking scheme. What does the examiner want to know *exactly*?

(i) Plan your answers

Some candidates are just not prepared to spend time on thinking and planning their answers. There is a temptation to write throughout the examination, and to write as much as possible, but this is usually a mistake. Planning is especially important in an examination because time is limited: as a result of spending some time on preparing a topic outline, all the remaining time can be used effectively (see Table 12.3).

Table 12.3 Allocating your time to a written answer

Activity	Time needed
Thinking about the question	3 min
Planning your answer	2 min
Writing (all the main points and enough explanation)	22 min
Checking	3 min

Without thought and planning, information and ideas will probably not be presented in the most effective order, information on one topic may be included in different parts of the answer, information may be repeated, too much detail may be included on some topics and not enough on others, essential topics may be omitted, and the answer as a whole is unlikely to be well balanced. Such disorganised answers give an unfavourable impression and are difficult to mark.

Remember that marks are awarded according to a marking scheme, for relevance, completeness, and understanding. You must therefore decide on a limited number of main points (topics for your paragraphs) that the examiner will expect you to deal with in the limited time available for your answer. Any irrelevant material is likely to be deleted by the examiner. The inclusion of irrelevant material is not only a waste of time but it also serves as a smoke-screen – making relevant parts of an answer harder to find.

Prepare a plan or topic outline for each answer. You may do this immediately before starting the answer. Alternatively, you may prefer to plan all your answers at the beginning of the examination so that you can reconsider each outline later – immediately before writing your answer.

Planning will help you to remember things; and your topic outline will help you to get started and give direction to your work (see page 72). Furthermore, additional points will come to mind as you write – according to plan.

You may decide to answer any compulsory questions first. Or you may answer first the questions you feel you can answer best. There are advantages in this, especially if you plan all your answers at the beginning of the examination, because it gives time for second thoughts about your other questions and you will probably benefit from reconsidering each question before you start to answer it.

However, you should take care not to spend more time on what you think are the easy questions (at the start of an examination) so that you have *less time* for other questions which may need *more thought*.

(j) Display your knowledge

Some candidates omit things because they consider them too elementary. However, in examinations you score marks by displaying knowledge and understanding. Basic facts and ideas should be included, even if briefly and in passing, at appropriate places.

Similarly, in numerical questions the stages in your calculation must be shown. The examiner can then give marks for the part of your working that is correct – even if the answer is wrong. If you simply give the wrong answer you can score no marks.

(k) Make clear your understanding

Some candidates include relevant material in their answers but do not score high marks because they fail to make clear their understanding. In advanced examinations, particularly, it is not usually enough to simply demonstrate that you have a good memory. You should show your intelligence by planning each answer so that you can select relevant information and ideas and present them in an effective order.

Show that you understand what is required in each part of your answer by using words from the question at appropriate points in your answer: perhaps you can use them in topic sentences or as subheadings. Show your understanding in each paragraph by starting with the main point you wish to make in this paragraph (in a direct and forceful topic sentence), by including *enough* evidence or *explanation* and, if appropriate, by giving an example.

Use each part of your answer, and each paragraph, as an *opportunity to score marks* by adding only relevant information and ideas, and by making clear your understanding.

(l) Cite sources

Pay sufficient attention, in your answers, to points emphasised in lectures and other classes – which your lecturers considered important – but as in coursework it is not usual to acknowledge these sources of information. However, you are advised to refer to relevant published work – citing sources as you would in course work. Examiners will recognise important contributions to their subject by the authors' names and the dates of publication, but you may wish to refer to some books by their titles as well as giving their authors' names. You will not be expected to remember full bibliographic details, so your answers to examination questions should not end with a bibliography or list of references cited.

(m) Arrange your answer for easy marking

Some candidates give a jumbled answer, so that it is difficult for the examiner to tell whether or not each part of the question has been answered. Remember that the examiner may have many scripts to mark. Try to make the task as easy as possible so that it is easy for the examiner to give the marks you have earned.

The different kinds of questions, which may be set in course work and examinations, must be tackled in different ways. If a question is set in parts you are advised to arrange the parts of your answer in the same order as they appear in the question (see page 181). Use letters (a), (b), (c), etc. if these are used in the question. Otherwise, select appropriate subheadings to act as signposts. This will help the examiner, who must work to a marking scheme (see page 120), to find and mark each part of your answer. It will also help you to ensure that you answer all parts of the question and allocate your time appropriately to each part.

In other types of questions, clear paragraph breaks should indicate that you have said all that you intend to say about one topic and are just about to start a new topic. By planning you can deal adequately with each topic in one place – and this makes marking easier.

Start each answer at the top of a new page, unless you are instructed to do otherwise, but do not leave gaps within an answer. For example, do not leave a gap at the bottom of a page and then continue your answer on the next page. If you do, the examiner may read the first part of your answer and give a mark, thinking that you have finished. Then, finding the additional material, the examiner has to read this to see if the mark should be altered.

(n) *Express your thoughts as clearly as you can*

Some students use more words than are needed to convey their intended meaning precisely, probably because they do not know much about the subject and are trying to make their limited knowledge go a long way. Perhaps they think that marks are given for the number of pages filled with writing.

On the contrary, words which convey no meaning are like hurdles in a race: they hinder the reader's progress and so make it harder for the writer to convey meaning. Instead of displaying what is known, the extra words obscure meaning and give the immediate impression that little or nothing is known.

Examiners see too much of such padded writing – full of superfluous words, gobbledegook, surplusage, verbosity – and are unlikely to be impressed by the outward show of an excess of words. They may be annoyed if they have to search for the meaning, or, being unwilling to do so, may skim through the answer and then give a low mark.

(o) *Write for easy reading*

Remember that marks are given for the content and quality of your answers – not for their length. Write complete and carefully constructed sentences so that your meaning is clear. Some candidates make mistakes in their choice of words, in spelling, punctuation and grammar, or write a careless scrawl. All these things contribute to ambiguity and create an immediately unfavourable impression.

Examiners can give marks only for what they can read. And they can give marks only for what is written – not for what they think the candidate probably meant.

(p) *Check your answers*

Some candidates complete their last answer just as the instruction is given to stop writing. They leave no time for checking their work.

If at all possible, leave yourself time to read through all your answers. Check that you have answered all parts of each question. Check that every word is legible. Correct any slips of the pen, obvious spelling mistakes, or sentences that do not make sense. Check calculations, including substitutions in formulae, algebraic and arithmetic operations, and the position of each decimal point. Check that the result of your calculation is a reasonable answer to the question asked.

By making corrections yourself you can avoid being penalized for the mistakes. You may also be able to score extra marks by adding important points that you did not remember previously, and without which your answer would be incomplete.

(q) Use your time effectively

Concentrate fully: do not allow your mind to wander.

If a diagram is needed do not include unnecessary lines or waste time on shading. Distinguish the parts of a diagram by using coloured pencils and by clear labelling.

Remember, if you make a mistake or have second thoughts, that the quickest way to delete a number, letter, word or paragraph is to draw one line through it. Delete with an oblique line through single letters and with a horizontal line through words, so that you have space for corrections between your lines of writing. Do not waste your time on rubbing out or using white correcting fluid: it is quicker to delete and write again.

Learn from your own mistakes

Sometimes, after an examination, you realise that you have not done your best work. Nothing is to be gained by worrying about this immediately. Put the examination out of your mind. Try to relax. If necessary, prepare for the next examination.

If your script is returned, after marking, consider the examiner's comments to see if you can learn from them. You may be able to improve your study, revision and examination techniques. Consider where you went wrong so that you can try to avoid making the same kind of mistake again. Note where you lost marks because you failed to express your meaning unambiguously. Learn by trying to correct your mistakes. Seek help if necessary.

If possible, look at better answers prepared by other students. And in later revision sessions, attempt the questions you did not answer in the examination.

Well prepared and ready to start

The day before an examination

1 Check again the date, time and location of your examination.
2 Prepare any writing materials or other equipment that you will need in the examination (e.g. pens with black or blue-black ink, sharp pencils, a ruler and an eraser, your watch, a calculator, and any books that you will be allowed to use).
3 If you decide to revise on the day before the examination do not work late.
4 Have a complete break, perhaps go for a walk, so that you can relax before going to bed.
5 Set your alarm clock *and make other arrangements* to ensure that you get out of bed in good time (Figure 12.1).
6 Try to have eight hours sleep. Relaxing on the day before, and a full night's sleep, will help you to be refreshed and alert

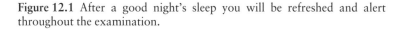

MAKE ARRANGEMENTS TO ENSURE THAT YOU GET OUT OF BED ON TIME

Figure 12.1 After a good night's sleep you will be refreshed and alert throughout the examination.

throughout the examination. This will do more good, in helping you to think clearly and score marks, than would too much last minute revision.

The day of an examination

1 Get up at the time you planned, so that you do not need to rush over washing and dressing, and you have time for a leisurely breakfast.
2 Check, before leaving, that you do have all the materials and equipment needed for the examination.
3 Arrive near to the examination room in good time but try to relax.
4 Go to the lavatory so that you will not need to leave the room during the examination.
5 Do not talk about the examination with other candidates.
6 Enter the examination room about ten minutes before the examination is due to start.
7 Find your place and arrange your writing materials and any other equipment on the working surface.
8 Write your name and other details, as instructed, in the spaces provided on the cover of your answer book.
9 If necessary, breathe in deeply – try to fill your lungs – then breathe out slowly. Do this a few times to help you to relax a little, but you should feel keyed up and ready to start.

Taking a theory examination

1 Read and *obey all the instructions* written on the front cover of your answer book. For example, you will probably be told to use a separate answer book for each part of the paper, to start each question at the top of a new sheet, and not to leave spaces within an answer or blank pages between the end of one answer and the start of the next.
2 *Check that you have been given the correct question paper*, that it is properly printed, and that you do have the whole paper.
3 *Read the instructions at the head of the paper.* Make sure you understand how much time is allowed, how many questions you should answer, and if there are any compulsory questions or any other restrictions on your choice.

4 *Read the whole paper* – all the questions – if you have a choice of questions. Look at both sides of each sheet to make sure that you do see all the questions.

5 *Select the questions that you can answer most fully*, then look again at the instructions at the head of the paper to check that your selection includes any compulsory questions and will be acceptable to the examiners.

6 *Allocate your time* to planning, writing and checking, so that you can do your best (i) to answer any compulsory questions; (ii) to answer the right number of questions, and (iii) to answer each question as fully as you are able in the time available for that question (see pages 178–80).

7 *Read each question again before you plan your answer.* Consider every word and phrase to make sure that you know exactly what the examiner wants to know, and for indications of the way the answer is to be presented (see page 137). Plan your answer (see page 71).

8 Before answering a question, write the number of the question conspicuously in the left hand margin at the top of a new page of your answer book, but *do not waste time copying out the question.*

9 You cannot spend much time on thinking about how to begin but a suitable starting point will probably become clear as you prepare the plan of your answer. In the first paragraph you will probably use some words from the question in a context which makes clear to the examiner that you do understand the question. Indeed, your first sentence or paragraph may give the essence of your answer.

10 Get to the point quickly and *keep to the point.* Work to your topic outline so that you can give an answer that is well balanced and well organised and so that you can make all your main points effectively in the time available – without digression or repetition (see page 115).

11 *Respond to the words used in the question* (see page 36). Do not make vague statements. Give reasons and examples. Include enough explanation.

12 Do not leave things out because you consider them too simple or too obvious (see page 183). *The examiner cannot assume that you know anything* and can give marks only for what you write.

13 If you include anything that is not obviously relevant, explain why it is relevant.

14 Use small letters – (a), (b) etc. – or subheadings, or distinct paragraph breaks, as appropriate, to *make clear to the examiner where one aspect of the question has been dealt with and the next part of your answer begins.*

15 If a question is set in several parts, you must *spend enough time on each part of your answer.* You should also do your best to answer the parts in the order in which they are set, because the examiner will prefer to mark them in this order.

16 If the number of marks allocated to each part of a question is shown, next to the question, this should indicate not only how much time you should devote to each part of your answer but also how many relevant points may be needed for an adequate answer to each part.

17 Make sure that any diagram is simple so that you can complete it quickly and neatly. Use coloured pencils, if necessary, to represent different things, but do not waste time on shading.

Each diagram should be in the most appropriate place but should be numbered so that you can refer to it in other parts of your answer. If diagrams are necessary they should complement your writing, making explanation easier and enabling you to present information and ideas that could not be adequately presented in words alone. Effective diagrams should therefore reduce the number of words needed in your answer. *Do not waste time by conveying the information in both words and a diagram.*

18 *Make sure that your writing is legible* and use black or blue-black ink. Remember that coloured ink may be mistaken for the examiner's corrections.

When you have completed your answer, and checked that you have included all points from your topic outline, it is a good idea to put a sloping line through your rough work so that the examiner can see at once that this is not part of your answer.

19 *Keep an eye on the time*, so that you can spend the right amount of time on each question (see page 179) and have time to check all your answers towards the end of the examination (see page 124).

20 Try to finish each question before starting the next, but if you get as far as you can with a question, or are unable to solve a problem, be prepared to leave it. Then remember to come back to it if

you have time after answering other questions. You may well make more progress at your second attempt.

21 *Do not leave before the end.* If you have checked your work and have time to spare, look at each question again and at your topic outline (Figure 12.2). Consider if there is anything you could add to improve any of your answers, so that you could score extra marks. Check that your name, and the other information required on the front page of your answer book, has been given.

22 When you leave the examination room nothing is to be gained from discussing the paper with other candidates. Try to think about other things, and to relax, until it is time to prepare for your next examination.

Taking a practical examination

Prepare for your practical examinations by looking through your reports on practical exercises completed during the course, and by revising relevant theory. Also remember in theory examinations, where appropriate, to refer to your practical experience.

DO NOT LEAVE BEFORE THE END

Figure 12.2 Make good use of all the time available in an examination.

In practical examinations the basic rules are similar to those stated for theory examinations.

1 Obey all instructions written on the front cover of your answer book, and at the head of the question paper.
2 Read all the questions.
3 Decide which questions you will answer – if you have a choice.
4 Decide the order in which you will tackle the questions, then
5 allocate your time, but remember . . .
6 In some practical examinations you may have time (e.g. while something is developing) to leave one question for a while and get on with another.
7 Also remember that you do not have to answer questions in the order in which they are set.
8 Read the question again before you start your answer, and follow any instructions carefully.
9 Spend as much time as is necessary on the easy questions – even if only a few marks are available for each of them. These few marks may help you to make a fail into a pass, or to make a good grade into a better one.
10 Make sure that your writing is legible and use black or blue-black ink.
11 Keep an eye on the time, and leave time to check all your answers towards the end of the examination.
12 Do not leave before the end.

Taking an oral examination

An oral or *viva voce* examination, after written examinations in any subject, may allow an examiner to explore your strengths and weaknesses. But be assured that although your grade may be raised as a result of this interview, you will not be down-graded.

Dress appropriately, to meet the examiner, and try to relax before the interview. Walk confidently into the room but do not sit until you are invited to do so. Then sit upright, so that you feel comfortable but alert. The examiner, after a friendly greeting, will ask your name – to make sure that you are the person expected at this time. As in normal conversation, be polite and self-confident but not aggressive. You must take the examination seriously but do smile occasionally: show your interest and enthusiasm. Be prepared to talk about your subject.

To give you time to relax, having read your extended essay or project report (based on your special study), the examiner may start by asking about this work. Speak clearly. Try not to answer simply yes or no. Give a little more information or explanation to show your knowledge and understanding, but do not go on for too long. If necessary give yourself time to think: you do not need to answer every question immediately. A few moments of thought and reflection may help you to collect your thoughts and summarise your reply. Leave the examiner free to ask further questions on this topic, or to move on to something else. If you do not understand any question, or are not quite sure exactly what the examiner wants to know, do not be afraid to ask.

Failing an examination

Heading for failure?

1 Do you attend all organised classes?
2 Do you review your notes soon after each class?
3 Are you doing appropriate background reading, using appropriate reading skills, and trying to fill gaps in your knowledge?
4 Do you ask for help when necessary?
5 Do you prepare for classes?
6 Do you revise regularly?
7 Do you complete all exercises set for homework, and hand them in for assessment on time?
8 Do you have difficulty in organising compositions or in expressing yourself clearly in writing?
9 Do you consider the comments and advice written on your assessed work?
10 Are you devoting enough time to all aspects of your subjects that will be assessed in course work and examinations?
11 Are you devoting enough time to recreation, and looking after yourself in other ways?
12 Are you working hard enough?

Assess your own progress. Are you likely to achieve a grade that is a true indication of your ability? If this self-evaluation causes you to decide that your performance is unsatisfactory, consider what you should do to bring about an improvement.

Failing

If you fail an examination, do not try to find excuses or to blame others. Perhaps you simply did not work hard enough, or did not make effective use of your study and leisure time, or did not revise regularly, or did not make effective use of your time in examinations. Recognising where you went wrong is the first step towards putting things right – if you decide to take the examinations again or to take some other course.

Perhaps you will decide to do something else and make new plans. However, do not make a hasty decision. First take a break and then reconsider your position.

Appendix A

Choosing a course

You probably studied a variety of subjects at school, as part of a broad education, and then selected certain subjects to take in examinations. Studying these subjects may have helped you to decide what to do next. More than this, it provided a foundation for your further studies. You would have encountered difficulties if you had decided, later, to work for a more advanced examination or to make a career in a field that is normally based on the study of other subjects.

These things are true at each stage in your formal education. If you wish to specialise in a particular subject in your later years at college, you may have to study this subject and others (called pre-requisites) in the earlier years. On the other hand, if you are not sure which is to be your main subject you should try to take a choice of subjects in the first year that will enable you to decide, later, to specialise in one or two of them.

Before starting any course of study, if you have a particular career in mind, talk to people who already have the qualification at which you are aiming. Also, look at the booklets on careers published, for example, by different professional bodies and institutes.

Consider what kind of course you should take and then find out what courses of this kind are available. You can do this by writing to the colleges at which you think you might like to study. Such enquiries should be made as far in advance of your preferred starting date as possible, so that you can complete your applications and submit them before any closing dates.

The entry requirements for advanced courses are such that, having satisfied them, you should be able to cope with the more advanced work. However, try to assess your suitability for this course. Read the information supplied by the college, and information about similar courses that may be available in your local library. If you are still at school, or studying part-time at a local college, your teachers will help you to understand what may be involved in further studies of their subjects. Otherwise, it is a good idea for anyone with a particular career in mind to talk to someone already qualified who has recently started upon such a career. Clearly, nothing is to be gained by attempting things for which you are not suited.

DISTANCE LEARNING

To be able to study in your own home may be an advantage, depending on your circumstances, but there are also disadvantages.

Disadvantages of distance learning

Notes prepared for you, by others, should not be as useful to you as your own lecture notes (see page 46). Also, there is more to be gained from lectures and other organised classes than a neat set of notes (see page 48). The home-based student may also suffer, both academically and socially, from lack of contact with other students.

At college the lecturers and other students help to set the pace. In distance earning (for example, in a correspondence course) you receive regular advice and instructions, and you will have to submit completed work for marking, but – even more than in other kinds of courses – the driving force must be yourself.

Self discipline is necessary. It is best to read quickly through the material, as soon as it arrives, and to consider what needs to be done. Then decide when you will do it. Make your own notes and leave space for additions when you undertake additional reading. Make notes of any difficulties or questions (see page 56). Start work on any exercises and plan to complete them in time (see Table 3.5, page 33).

The main problem for the distance learner is isolation. There is no one you can easily turn to for advice, except in so far as the librarians in your local library are able to help. However, some distance learning courses are so organised that students can meet their tutors and other students living locally (see also e-mail, page 103, and e-learning, page 105) and attend short residential courses.

Advantages of distance learning

1 Distance learning courses are available to anyone and some require no previous experience of knowledge of the subject. So you can start at the beginning and build on the foundations provided early in your course.
2 Distance learning is particularly attractive to people who live in remote areas, or are unable to attend a college regularly because of family ties or incapacity, or cannot attend college full time and live in places where there is no suitable part-time course available.
3 Time can be devoted to study instead of to travel.
4 You can choose your own time for study, in relation to other commitments such as full-time employment.
5 You can work at your own pace.
6 You are provided with notes that will help you to prepare for a particular examination; and if you are not very good at note-making these may be better than your own notes would be.
7 There may be relevant broadcast films and talks, and some of these may be designed to support the course you are taking.
8 Regular set work is planned for you. If you keep up with your work, week by week, your progress is monitored and you receive comments and advice.
9 Distance learning courses give a second chance or an opportunity for further education for people who are already employed, but before undertaking such a course consider what will be involved and what other demands there will be on your time. Determination will be needed and there is no point in starting any course unless you are prepared to find the time that will be required.

STUDYING PART-TIME

The main advantage of part-time study is that you can start upon a career and continue your education at the same time. Part-time attendance also enables students, who for one reason or another cannot take a full-time course, to continue their education, meet lecturers and other students who have similar interests to their own, ask for advice, use facilities, and obtain qualifications that will help them to make progress in their careers. Part-time courses also enable qualified people to obtain further or higher qualifications in the early years of their subsequent employment or to take refresher courses after they have been employed for some years. However, part-time study is more demanding than full time study, it is likely to leave less time to devote to personal relationships and recreation – and is not to be entered into lightly.

Part-time study and distance learning is particularly attractive to people who already have many commitments (for example, full-time or part-time employment, a house to maintain, children to care for). Such people, before committing themselves to study, should decide whether or not they will find the time that will be needed to attend all classes (see page 45) and for private study (see page 28). Are they prepared to give up other things? Will they receive cooperation and encouragement from their family or friends, which will be necessary if they are to have (a) regular free evenings or week-ends to attend organised classes, (b) time to visit libraries, and (c) periods of quiet study?

STUDYING FULL-TIME

If you decide upon a full-time course, consider what type of course to take. Most full-time courses include periods of attendance at college (in term time) and periods away from college (in vacations); but in cooperative education or sandwich courses, periods of full-time attendance at college alternate with periods of training in relevant paid employment. Such courses take longer (perhaps four years instead of three). Apart from the longer time needed, you may have difficulty in settling down at college after a long break in your studies. Therefore, the period of appropriate employment should be regarded not as a break in your studies but as an opportunity to relate college work to a particular career. Some time in the evenings and at week-ends should still be devoted to the revision and consolidation of college work and to background reading. If these opportunities are taken, the habit of studying is not lost during the training period; and you return to college with a good basis for the next year of the course.

If asked what you hoped to gain from a period of further or higher education, you would probably reply that you wanted to obtain a particular qualification. You might add that you intended to do as well as possible in your final examinations. To obtain employment you would also need a good reference or recommendation from your Head of Department or from another senior member of the academic staff of your college. If you take a course that includes periods of relevant paid employment you will gain experience, learn to get along with people, become more self-reliant away from home or college, and so gain in maturity of outlook. You will also hope to obtain a good reference or recommendation from a senior member of staff at the training establishment, when the time comes to look for permanent employment.

Appendix B

Computer appreciation

USING YOUR COMPUTER

Many people hand-write at least the first draft of anything other than a very short composition so that they can work fast enough to allow their thoughts and their written words to flow. Then they spend more time than should be necessary word processing later drafts.

So, if you cannot touch type it is worth learning, preferably before using a computer for word processing. You could attend a class on keyboard skills, or buy a computer program that provides on-screen instruction, or learn from a book that includes basic instructions and graded exercises. With regular and frequent practice, you should soon be typing faster than you can write.

Word processing

With appropriate software you can use a personal computer to produce pages of text, including tables and illustrations, with a print quality similar to that of a book. However, your work will be easier to read if you do not justify right hand margins, or use bold, italics or underlining to emphasise words (except that italic print is used for the words *either* and *or* if it is necessary to emphasise an important distinction). Italics, or underlining, should also be used for words that in a hand-written composition would be underlined (see page 125). Capitals, bold print and italics can be used for different grades of headings (see page 116, but because most headings should be given a line to themselves – for emphasis – there is no need to underline them.

If some users think of a word processor as a tool that eliminates the need for thinking and planning before writing, and for care in writing, because it is easy to correct and revise their work later, they are wrong. A computer has a memory but no intelligence. It is a tool that can make writing easier, but the writer still has to do the thinking at each stage in composition.

When working on a screen, as in writing with a pen, you must: (a) make notes as you think about what is required, (b) re-arrange your notes below appropriate headings as you prepare a topic outline for your composition, (c) choose and arrange words carefully as you write to ensure you express your thoughts clearly and simply, and then (d) check, correct and if necessary revise your work (see pages 124–5). As a result, there should not be much wrong with your first draft. If there is, nothing you can do in checking and revising can compensate for your not having considered the needs of the reader, or for not devoting enough time to thinking and to planning, before starting to write. This is true whether your composition is hand-written or word-processed.

Because with a word processor it is so easy to make additions and deletions, to cut and paste, and to copy, great care is needed in checking a document to ensure that it reads well, with no words missing and no words, sentences or paragraphs duplicated or out of place.

Use the spell checker on your computer. It will help you to correct typing errors and spelling mistakes, and so to improve your spelling. However, although a spell checker ensures that each word used is spelt correctly (in American English or British English) it does not ensure that it is the right word. For example, does the spelling and grammar checker on your computer draw attention to any errors when you type the following sentences?

> I advice you to consider the following advise.
> There's too mistakes in the last sentence.

There are, in fact, two mistakes in each of the sentences. They should read:

I advise you to consider the following advice.

There're two mistakes . . . (There's is a contraction of There is)

However, in scholarly writing it is best to avoid such contractions by writing:

There are two mistakes . . .

Also, do not allow a spell checker to spell-check and change, automatically, specialist terms, abbreviations, acronyms, or proper names (of people and places) unless these are correct in your computer's spell-check dictionary. It would be embarrassing, for example, if the computer changed Mr Charlton's surname to Charlotte or worse to Charlatan – and you did not notice the mistake when checking the document.

You may be required to use a word processor for some of your course work assignments, but if you word process them all you may find in examinations, when you have to use handwriting, that you cannot do your best work, because: (a) you cannot write fast enough, (b) you have very little time in which to check each composition, (c) you cannot use a spell checker, and (d) it is not possible to rearrange your material.

In course work you can devote more time on thinking and planning than you could spare in an examination but, to give yourself regular practice with pen and paper, at least the first draft of your answer should be hand-written in about the time that would be available in an examination – when you would not be able to use a word processor.

Furthermore, in course work students who can prepare a neat hand-written first draft that is legible and well presented – so that it does not need to be revised – should not be required, as they are on many courses, to waste their time word processing a second draft just to change their handwriting into print. Your assessors should be impressed by what you say and by good presentation (and all that this involves, see Table 8.2) but should not be deceived by outward show – by mere ornament.

As a student you must develop the ability to produce a good hand-written composition quickly and get things right the first time – *as you have to in examinations* – so that your first draft needs only minor corrections. And both students and their assessors should accept that a composition can be well presented in course work – as in examinations – without its being word processed (see page 125).

Looking after your documents

1 Information obtained via the Internet, including attachments to incoming e-mail messages, might be contaminated with viruses, and should be checked before opening.

2 Before using a computer, therefore, ensure that it has up-to-date virus-detecting and virus-removing software installed.

3 Before using a disk for the first time, ensure that it is checked with an up-to-date virus checker.

4 When producing a new document, use a new disk and backup disk for just that document.

5 Save (or file) your work frequently, as you plan, write, correct, or revise a document, so that if anything is lost (for example, as a result of a power failure) you do not lose much of the document and can try to do the work again quickly while the information and ideas are still fresh in your mind.

6 Save your work before you try any new commands if there is any possibility that you may lose or inadvertently alter part or all of the document, so that you can quit (that is, leave the document in its original state) and try again.

7 Your floppy disks may go wrong, as may the hard disk of your personal computer, causing you to lose all your work at any time. So ensure that all data stored in a computer are backed up with a frequency that reflects their value and importance. Take a local copy immediately after data have been entered from memory, or from an enquiry or investigation. Each day, when working on a document, make a new copy using a different file name (for example, the year, month, and day). If you are working on a document for several days, or for several weeks, take daily, weekly and monthly backups on separate disks. Bear in mind that disks are inexpensive, whereas your time spent in re-entering lost information – if this were possible – would cost much more and would interfere with your other work.

8 Label your disks consecutively (for example, with your initials and a number: ABC001, ABC002, etc.) and maintain a log of your disks in a small hardback notebook. Record what each

disk contains, and for backup disks record the type of backup (daily, weekly, or monthly).

9 When a document is complete, copy it into your master archive disk, and backup archive disk, in case you need copies later, or need to update it, or include parts in another document.

10 Reformat your document disk ready for your next document.

11 Do not carry all your disks with you at one time. Keep your master archive and master back-up disks in separate places, so that if one is lost or damaged you still have the other.

Looking after yourself when using a computer

1 Sit comfortably at your computer. Adjust your chair so that you are close to the desk, with your elbows level with the computer keyboard, your feet resting flat on the floor or on a foot rest, and your back upright. When using a mouse, rest your arm on the desk and move your hand by moving the elbow rather than the wrist. If you touch type, you could try using a contoured keyboard.

2 Adjust the height of the visual display unit, if necessary, so that your eyes are level with the top of the screen and 30 to 60 cm from the screen.

3 Ensure the screen is clean and free from glare (for example, from a lamp or window) and that the keyboard and your working surface are sufficiently illuminated – but have a matt surface that does not reflect light.

4 If necessary, adjust the brightness and contrast controls on your visual display unit, so that the background is no brighter than is necessary for you to see the words clearly.

5 If you cannot touch type you will find it tiring to be constantly looking down at the keyboard, and at your hand-written draft, and then up at the screen. But if you can touch type you will not need to look at the keyboard when copy typing and may find it helpful to use a document holder to hold your papers adjacent to the screen.

6 Do not allow the use of a computer to become an end in itself. A computer helps you to do many things, some of which would not otherwise be possible (for example, in recording, processing, storing, and retrieving information); but in study and at work much time can also be wasted in fruitless activity. When seeking information, try to find just the information you need as quickly

as possible. When word processing, take care at all stages in the preparation of a document – but recognise when it will serve its purpose and the job is done.

7 As an aid to concentration, work to a job list (see page 34) and organise your work so that you engage in different activities. In particular, it is not a good idea to sit still – staring at a screen – for long periods. Take a break of at least five minutes in every hour – exercising, relaxing, or working in a different way. This will help you to concentrate and will reduce fatigue.

Although you may be able to make more use of your computer to help you with your writing, you are advised to organise your work so that you spend no more time than is necessary actually sitting and looking at the screen.

MAKING MORE USE OF YOUR COMPUTER

Many who use a computer for word processing, for sending and receiving e-mail, and for obtaining information via the Internet, do not appreciate how they can use it in other ways to help them with their writing – with software programs that may already be installed in their computers. Although a program was developed to help users perform a particular task (for example, word processing) it may be installed as part of a suite containing other programs developed to help users with other tasks (for example, with drawing diagrams and charts, with desk top publishing, with preparing and delivering presentations, and with preparing and using spreadsheets and databases); and each of these programs may have capabilities that overlap with those of the others.

Desk top publishing

With desk top publishing software, page layouts can be planned in a choice of formats, with tables and figures in appropriate places close to relevant text. The result should be a finished appearance indistinguishable from pages in a printed newsletter, magazine, book, or other publication. With improvements in word processing software, however, the line between word-processing (with a word processing program) and desk-top publishing (with a desktop publishing program) is increasingly difficult to draw, and anyone

considering preparing camera ready copy for a publisher should
ascertain the publisher's requirements before starting to write.

Preparing presentations

With appropriate software it is easy to prepare: (a) a topic outline
for a talk, (b) speaker's notes, (c) visual aids for use during the talk
as overhead projector transparencies or as slides, and (d) handouts
providing further details – for distribution after a talk. Slides
(images stored electronically on a disk) can be prepared with or
without a background colour and design; and both visual aids and
handouts can include words alone, tables, charts, or other artwork –
including photographs. However, care should be taken that the
choice of background, or the use of special effects, is not such as to
distract listeners – who should be concentrating on your message.

Using spreadsheets

In a spreadsheet data are entered in a table in which vertical ruled
lines between the columns and horizontal ruled lines between the
rows form a grid in which the resulting spaces are called cells.
Whereas in a printed table, on a page, the number of columns and
rows is limited by the type size used and by page size, a spreadsheet
can be much larger – according to your needs. You can store data in
cells and by entering appropriate formulae in other cells you can
perform calculations, analyse numerical data, and obtain statistics,
as with a calculator. Furthermore, data saved on a disk can be edited
and if you need to change an entry or add data in extra cells, or even
add or delete whole columns or rows of data, recalculations are
completed almost immediately and automatically by the computer.
You do not have to calculate or recalculate.

Spreadsheets can be used for keeping records of your personal
finances, and in business, for example, for recording and analysing
sales data, and for accounts. As in word processing, spreadsheets
can be printed as hard copy, and if necessary can be incorporated
in word-processed documents. Results of the analysis of data,
recorded on spreadsheets, can also be used to produce graphs, his-
tograms and charts, and these too can be incorporated in word-
processed documents (or in the handouts and visual aids used in
presentations).

Preparing and using a database

With appropriate software, it is easy to construct and maintain a database – in which data are recorded electronically in a table and stored in a computer. Advantages of an electronic database are that: (a) it occupies less space than would a filing cabinet or card index used to store the same information, (b) records can be sorted easily and quickly – and data extracted – according to one's immediate needs, (c) it is easy to add, correct and delete records to keep them up-to-date. However, most students are likely to use folders and filing boxes for their notes, and index cards for their bibliographic records (see page 63).

Databases are most useful in administration, business and management when many people need access to the same data. A database then has the additional advantage that records are not lost or incorrectly filed – and so unavailable – as a result of the carelessness of some users.

Some people confuse spreadsheets with databases, but there is very little overlap in their applications: a spreadsheet is not a database. When planning a database, as when preparing a table, before entering any data you must decide the column headings to be used. In a database these headings are called field names. They indicate the kinds of information to be kept – in relation, for example, to each person or each item listed in the first column (called the stub in a table). In staff records, for example, the column headings would include: Surname, First name, Employee ID (the primary key: a unique identifying alphanumeric reference), Date employed, Post held, Department, and Salary.

In a database it is easy to amend records: to add or delete horizontal rows of cells (for example, in one database – as staff join or leave the business, or in another – as new kinds of goods are added to stock or as other kinds are sold out and not replaced), and to change the information in any cell (as, for example, people are moved from one department to another, or as the stock of each product changes from day to day).

However, adding columns (fields) is impossible with some databases and can cause problems with others. So the specification for a database must be carefully considered, and a business practice or procedure may have to be better defined, before the specification for the database can be written. Then the database must be prepared by someone who understands the uses of a database.

The kind of database described here, in which operations are performed in one table, is called a flat file system. In another kind of database, called a relational database system, different tables can be linked by common fields so that when changes are made in one they are also made automatically, at the same time, in the others. This saves space in the database, eliminates duplication of effort – in data collection and data entry – and so saves time, and ensures that everyone using the database has access to identical data.

Databases can be constructed so as to provide different levels of data protection. For example, in an organisation some people may be able to view a particular screen showing personnel data complete (including personal details) whereas other employees accessing the same screen would not see such sensitive information.

People with good software skills should be able to design and construct a simple database, using a desktop PC program, but server databases and mainframe databases are designed by specialist database engineers.

PURCHASING A COMPUTER

Anyone selecting and purchasing a computer is likely to have conflicting requirements, so some cannot be completely satisfied. Some conflicting requirements result from the increasing rate of technological change. For example, obsolescence may make it desirable to update software as soon as possible, but because of the costs involved in purchasing new software and in acquiring new skills it may be necessary to delay making changes.

In relation to both the cost of purchasing a computer system and the decision as to the best time to buy, one should also bear in mind that any computer or information technology equipment you are thinking of buying will cost less, or will be obsolete and replaced by a more powerful and cheaper system, if you wait. The longer you wait, the better value you may expect to obtain for your money. In particular, if you are thinking of purchasing a new personal computer before starting a college or university course, it is advisable to wait to see what facilities are available at your college or university, to benefit from any advice, and to find out if there are any special requirements for your course.

Appendix C

Further reading

BOOKS FOR YOUR BOOKSHELF

1 Look at the books included in your reading lists, and at other recommended publications, as suggested on page 86. Be prepared to buy up-to-date textbooks for each aspect of your course. Make sure that each one is appropriate for your course and for the stage you have reached in your studies. If there is a choice, select books which you find easy to read and understand. Your lecturers will be pleased to offer advice; and you may find it helpful to talk to students who passed the course last year.

You will need a good textbook from the start of each course of lectures. It will complement the lectures and should be on your bookshelf – available for preliminary reading before lectures and for immediate reference.

2 Buy a dictionary that gives the spelling, pronunciation and meaning of each word, its uses in current English, its derivatives (words derived from it), and its derivation: for example, *Chambers' Twentieth Century Dictionary* (Chambers, Edinburgh), *Collins' Dictionary of the English Language* (Collins, Glasgow), *The Concise Oxford Dictionary of Current English* (Oxford University Press, London), and *Websters' New Collegiate Dictionary* (Merriam, Massachusetts).

3 Many students are clever enough to understand their work and yet unable to organise and communicate their thoughts

effectively. They need help with their writing more than further instruction in their chosen subjects. If you have found this book helpful, and accept that you need further help with your writing, study these handbooks: Barrass, R. (1995) *Students Must Write: a guide to better writing in course work and examinations*, 2nd edn, Routledge, London and New York. Gowers, E. (1986) *The Complete Plain Words*, 3rd edn revised by Greenbaum, S. & Whitcut, J, HMSO, London.

4 For an audio-visual introduction to study techniques, see: Main, A.N. (1987) *Study Patterns,* in list of References (page 211).

5 If you have a study problem and need help or further advice, see a member of the academic staff or a study counsellor at your college (see pages 14 and 22).

If you wish to discuss a personal problem see your personal tutor or academic adviser, or any other member of the academic staff whom you find approachable and sympathetic (see page 22). You will find that most teachers accept that counselling is part of their work and are pleased to help.

If you need advice on a medical problem, or treatment for any disease or illness, see your doctor without delay.

Lecturers and tutors, who meet students regularly and are frequently asked for advice on study and personal problems, will find many helpful suggestions in: Main, A.N. (1980) *Encouraging Effective Learning: an approach to study counselling*, Scottish Academic Press, Edinburgh.

References

Hanson, H. R. (1963) *The Concept of the Positron*, Cambridge, Cambridge University Press.

Howard, M. (1981) 'The Lessons of History': an inaugural lecture at the University of Oxford: reprinted in Howard, M. (1991) *The Lessons of History*, Oxford, Oxford University Press.

Main, A. (1987) *Study Patterns*, Video presentations 'Listening Skills', 'Reading Skills' and 'Writing Skills' (and, 1991, 'If you are a Mature Student'), Glasgow, University of Strathclyde.

Orwell, G. (1946) Politics and the English Language, *Horizon* No. 76 (April, 1946): reprinted in Orwell, G. (1957) *Selected Essays*, Harmondsworth, Penguin Books, 143–157.

Quiller-Couch, A. (1916) *On the Art of Writing*, Cambridge, Cambridge University Press.

Read, Miss (1959) *Thrush Green*, London, Michael Joseph.

Schaefer, J (1954) *Shane*, London, Andre Deutsch.

Walpole, H. (1919) *Jeremy*, London, Macmillan.

Index

abbreviations 50–1, 140
ability 7, 12, 13, 15, 25
abstracts 102
accommodation 10, 16
acknowledgements 112, 152
active and passive verbs 135
advice: asking for 14, 21–2, 98, 105, 129; considering 129; of supervisor 147, 149, 150, 156
aims: *see* goals; *see also* purpose
answers: *see* questions
anxiety: avoiding 12–22, 23–41; before examinations 161, 171, 176, 187
appendices: use of 153
arrangement: *see* order
assertion 156
assessment 124, 126, 175; by self 125; continuous 126, 175; of composition 120, 121; of course work 109, 127; of examinations 109, 127; feedback on 126; grading criteria 121; *see also* grades, marking scheme, marks
assignments: *see* course work, special study
Association (and learning) 117, 118
assumption 156
attendance 45–6, 57, 171
authority 112

balance 116

beginning: *see* introduction
bias 81–2, 90, 91, 114
bibliographic details 91–2, 100, 184, record of 91–2, 155–6; *see also* citing sources
bibliography 92, 112, 113, 184

calculations 84
Career: advice on 195; progress in 9, 197
cheating 112, 126
checking: answers 124–5, 185–6; composition 125, 160; class notes 31, 58, 61; topic outline 31, 35, 120
circumlocution 135, 185
citing sources 92, 112–13, 152, 173, 183
clarity 131, 185
cliché 135
common skills 9, 43
communication skills 9, 59
comparison 137
composition: checking 124, 125; common faults in 110–17; creativity 117–19; planning 31, 33, 71–5, 153–4; writing 117–22; *see also* creativity
comprehension 96
computer: appreciation 200–8; assisted instruction/learning 105–8; conferencing 63; purchasing 208; using 204–5

concentration: in study 36–41, 48, 67, 90; on observation 79

conclusion: of argument 113; of composition 132; section of report 152

confidence: *see* self confidence

cooperative education 198

copies (need for) 155

Copying: from books 67, 102, 112–15; from other people 112, 126; own work 84

core skills 9, 43

correlation (cause and effect) 84, 114

counselling services 22

course: assessment 124–8, 163; choice of 195–8; content 46, 50, 165; guide (outline) 24, 46–7, 164, 165; plan 24; requirements 163–4; work 43, 109–17, 124–8, 129, 164, 202; unit (module) xiii; *see also* homework

cramming 76

creativity 117–19, 128

criticism 137; of own work 124, 130; of published work 89–91

data: analysing 83, 84, 155, 206; recording 79, 82–4, 155, 206; sheets 83, 155

databases 207–8

definitions 110, 137, 139–40, 170

description 137

desk top publishing 205–6

diagrams 111, 169, 170; in report 157; preparing 206

dictionaries 99, 209

diet 16

difficulties (coping with) 5, 13, 14, 22

digression 114

discussion: in speaking 59–63; in writing 137; section of report 152, 155

dissertation 147, 151, 155, 160

distance learning 43, 63, 196–7

dogma 82, 114

double negatives 135

drugs 18–20

education (purpose of) 126, 175

effort 5, 13, 28, 31

e-learning (on-line instruction) 103

e-mail 63

emphasis: in speaking 50; in writing 116, 120

employment: as career 25, 26; as student 25, 31

encyclopaedias 100

English: colloquial, slang and standard 136; *see also* language

enquiry: *see* investigation

enterprise skills 9, 43

essay writing: *see* composition; *see also* questions

evaluation 137

evidence 111, 114, 120

examinations 126; avoiding anxiety 176; failing 193–4; learning from 186; oral 192–3; past papers 166; practical 191–2; preparing for 161, 163–72; taking 176–86, 188–91; technique 176–93; written 176–91; *see also* revision

examples 111, 120

exercise and health 15–16

exercises and discussion topics: aids to study 34, 48, 70, 91–6; aids to thinking 71–2, 75–6; analysing questions 136–7; asking for help 14, 22, 56–7, 98–9, 196; being a student 24–5, 163–4; continuous assessment 126; contributing to a discussion 59–63; criticising a composition 122–4, 133–4; effective study 36–41, 75–6; examination technique 176–86; explaining 110, 137; goals and tasks 3, 38–9; how to remember 67–70; how to revise 68–9, 75–61, 161, 163–73; keeping records 63–5, 203–4; making notes (*see* notes); making observations (*see*

observation); planning answers
(*see* questions); preparing a
definition 139–40; preparing a
dissertation (*see* special study);
preparing an essay (*see*
composition); preparing a précis
(*see* précis); preparing a project
report 151, 152; preparing a
summary (*see* summary);
preparing a talk 142–6;
preparing a term paper 151, 160;
purpose of practical work 77–84;
reading critically 89–91; reading
faster 89; rules for study 8,
36–41; schedules (timetables)
28–33; study habits 36–41;
testing yourself 169; writing
faster 141
experience 5, 90, 91, 169
explanation 71, 137

facts 77, 114, 156
fatigue 38, 39
feedback 126, 129, 130, 164
filing notes 64–5
financial problems 11–12, 22
food and health 16
free periods (use of) 31
friendship 16–22, 63
full-time study 10, 27–8, 43, 198–9
fundamentals 5, 47, 58, 66, 68

goals (aims, objectives) 3–5, 9, 21,
37
grades 13, 27, 124
grammar 124
group work 43, 59–63

handbooks 100, 210
handouts 54, 58–9
handwriting 141–2, 202
headings: in composition 116–17,
132, 151, 152–3, 154, 159, 201;
in essay 116; in notes 52, 93;
hierarchy of 154; numbering of
154
health 12–22
help: *see* advice

homework 164; *see also*
assessment, course work

ideas: preconceived 81–2; reading
for 85, 88, 91; sources of 112, 119
illustration 137
imagination 117, 120
index cards 65, 144, 156, 167–8,
207
indexing journals 102
information: finding 9, 42, 100,
103, 104; sources of 59, 85–91,
96, 98–108, 112–13, 118; storing
63–5, 203–4; retrieval systems
102, 156
information technology 98
intelligence 12, 13, 15, 25
interest: developing 5–6, 14, 49
interests (non-academic) 25–6
Internet 102–4
Intranets 104
introduction: to composition 132;
section of report 152, 155
investigation: observing 77–83;
report on 83–4, 147
issues 157
italics (use of) 125

job list 34, 205
journals 101

key skills 9, 43
knowledge 85; acquiring 75, 77,
85; displaying 110, 111–13, 183;
filling gaps in 110, 117;
organising 116–19; recognising
gaps 35, 71, 166, 174; using 70;
see also learning, remembering,
understanding

language: appropriate 119–120;
colloquial 136; correct use of
131, 135–6; inappropriate 114;
slang 136; standard 136
learning: active (*see* study), aids to
48, 67, 96; basis for 67, 118; by
rote 66, 69, 98; computer based
105–8; from mistakes 1, 177–86;

objectives/outcomes 24, 46, 164, 165, 174, 175; opportunities for 48, 59; programmed 105–8; responsibility for 1, 23–4, 43, 173; student centred 26, 43; *see also* remembering, revising, study, understanding

lectures: attending 45–6; preparing for 47, purpose of 46, 48–9; review of 58; value of 46–9; *see also* notes

leisure: 13; effective use of 15–16, 17, 25, 26, 28, 31, 40–1; misuse of 15

library: access to catalogues 103; classification systems 100–1; place to study 11, 31

literature survey 101, 156

logic 113

loneliness: *see* friendship

manuscript (first draft) 154, 200

marking scheme 120, 149, 150, 181, 182; *see also* assessment, grades

marks: scoring 114, 121, 126, 132, 137, 147, 178–80, 184

memorising: *see* remembering

memory 13, 46, 69–70, 144

mistakes: correcting 124–5, 160, 186; learning from 1, 177, 186

mnemonics 70

module (course unit) xiii

module guide 24, 46, 165

money management 9, 11–12

motivation 24, 25

notes 45–6; care of 64, 65; central place in study 50, 96; checking 58; copying 58; creative pattern 53–4, 57; for composition (*see* topic outline); for guidance 151; for revision 167–9; from books 91–6; from lectures 45–59; linear (sequential) 51–3, 58; making 45–6, 48, 49–50, 60, 63–4, 91–6,

132; of observations 82–3, 84; one set 95–6

noun: abstract and concrete 135; definition 140

objectives: *see* goals

objectivity 120

observation 77–84; aids to 78; difficulties 78–82

on-line learning 103

open learning 105

opinion 90, 91, 102, 111, 114, 156

order 119; of headings 116, 152–3; of observations 119; of paragraphs 72–5, 116, 117, 154

organisation: of composition 116 (*see also* topic outline); of studies 12, 24, 27, 28, 34, 38–41; of thoughts 70–1

originality 115, 129–30

outline 137; *see also* topic outline

overwork 12

over-learning 161

paragraphs 72, 73, 74, 132, 151, 154

part-time study 10, 11, 28, 43, 63

periodical 101, 102

personal computer 63, 102, 105

personal development 17, 25, 43, 175

personal organiser 34

personal problems 21–2

personal relationships 20–1

personal skills 9, 43

persuasion 91

photocopying 92

plagiarism 67, 112, 126

planning: answers 71–5, 137–9, 182; composition 72, 116–19, 120, 128

posture 37, 111

practical work 67, 77–84

précis writing 96–7

prejudice (bias) 81–2, 90, 91, 114

preparation: before class 47, 48, 57, 59, 61, 62; before investigation 78; before writing (see topic outline); for discussion 61; for examination (see revision); for talk (presentation) 61, 142–4

presentation: of composition 124, 125, 202; talk 61, 146, 206

pre-requisites 5, 195

priorities (order of) 13, 28, 34–6

problem for investigation 14, 21–2, 155; *see also* difficulties

progress: guide to 164; report of 156

project report 152–3, 155, 160; *see also* special study

proposition 155

public speaking 142

punctuation 124

purpose: of composition 128; of education 126; of lecturer 50; in practical work 84; in reading 86–8, 90; in writing 120; *see also* goals

qualifications 25, 195–6, 198

questions: analysing 137–9; answering 33, 70–5, 117–22, 137, 141, 166–7; asking 14, 24, 48, 56–7, 60, 61, 87; of reader 72, 151; selecting 166–7, 177–8; spotting 172, 180; structured 181; understanding 136–40; words use in 136–7

quotations 112

rapid reading 89

reader (needs of) 136–7, 157–8, 185

reading: background 112, 117, 165; before class 47, 48, 56, 57, 59; before writing 112; critically 89–91; good English 141; how to read 13, 86–96; lists 13, 86; questions 137–9; what to read 86–7; see also information

recall techniques 72

recreation: need for 12, 15, 24–6, 171; opportunities for 17, 24–5; time for 24–6, 33, 171

reference publications 98–100

references (list of sources) 92, 112, 113, 153, 184

relaxation 14–16, 17, 18, 28

relevance: in reading 90; in writing 111, 114, 116, 180–1

remembering 13, 76, 98; aids to 48, 58–9, 67, 70; in study 59, 66–76

repetition: in composition 91, 115–16, 157; and remembering 48, 67–9, 75; in talk 143

report: on investigation 84, 147; parts of 152–3; of progress 156

responsibility 10, 24, 31

results 83, 84

review: after class 57, 58–9, 61; articles 101; part of study 40, 68, 94, 95, 161

revision: after class 59, 61, 98; after reading 94, 95; aids 167–9; of composition 124, 125; for examination 161, 163–73; notes for 167–9; part of study 27, 34, 39, 68–9, 75; spacing 27, 34, 69, 75; *see also* remembering

rote learning 66, 69, 98

sandwich courses (cooperative education) 198

satisfaction 13, 35, 40, 67, 128,

schedule (timetable) 28–33

school and college (differences) 23–4

self confidence 17, 176; in speaking 59

self expression 128, 131

self discipline 9

self-help groups 62–3

self reliance 17

seminars 60–1

sentences 132–3

set work: *see* course work

simplicity 120

skim reading 87, 88, 90

sleep 16, 18

sources of information: citing 92, 112–13, 153, 173, 183; primary and secondary 101

special study 43; assessing 147–8, 149; finding information for 148, 156; *see also* information; notes

for guidance 151–7; report on
151–6, 157–60; selecting subject
for 147–8; supervision 149–51;
terms of reference for 148, 150,
152
specialist terms 136, 139–40, 158
speculation 114, 157
spelling 124; check 201–2
spreadsheets 206
storing: disks 203–4; index cards
65; notes 64–5
stress: *see* anxiety
student centred learning 97
study: active 48, 57, 61, 67–9, 71,
75, 87, 90, 94, 109, 166, 168–70;
approach to 24, 31, 35; breaks in
13, 39; concentrating on 36–41,
67, 90; conditions for 11, 36–8;
counselling 14, 21–2; effective 6,
12, 14, 25, 36, 66; full-time 10,
27–8, 43, 198–9; groups 59–63;
organising 27–41; part time 10,
11, 28, 43, 63, 198; problems 14;
returning to 10; rules for 8;
satisfaction from 13, 128, 167;
skills 7–9, 43 (*see also* exercises);
tasks 13, 34–6, 38–9; techniques
164
subheadings 132
success (basis for) 12, 15, 24
summarising 9, 97–8
summary: of answer/composition
132; section of report 152
syllabus 46, 85, 165

tables 54–5, 157
talk (presentation) 61, 142–6
team work 63
technical terms: 136, 139–40, 158
term paper 147, 151, 160 (*see also*
special study)
terms of reference: for talk 143; for
report 148
terms of subject 136, 139–40, 158
tests: preparing for 161; taking
174–6
textbooks 46, 98, 165
things to do 34, 205

thinking: about questions 61, 71–2,
115, 117–19; and learning
66–76; and planning 201
time: effective use of 119; for
recreation 15–16, 17; for sleep
16; for study 28–36; ineffective
use of 110; management 4, 5, 9,
23–41, 154, 159; use in
examinations 178–80, 186; use
in tests 175; wasting 31
timetable (schedule) 28–33
topic: of paragraph 72, 132; outline
60, 61, 73, 117, 120–2, 130, 140,
172, 182; sentence 132, 154
transferable skills 9, 43
tutorials 59–60
typescript 158–160

under-achievement 9, 14, 23, 45–6,
110, 127–8, 163, 176
underlining 125
understanding: basis for 66;
developing 118, 128, displaying
110–11; in reading 96; questions
71, 136–9

vacations 27
visual aids 144–6

web pages 102
word processing 154, 155,
200–5
words: choice of 134, 135–6;
length of 134; meaning of
136–40; number of 134–5; of
question 136–7; of subject 136,
139–40; superfluous 134–5, 185;
use of 131
worry (anxiety) *see* stress
writing: and learning 71–6,
128–30; and reading 91–8;
answers to questions 71–6,
117–21; checking 124–5;
common faults in 110–17;
imaginative 119; importance of
109; judged by 109, 121, 126–8;
materials 63–5, 120, 142;
scholarly 120; when to start 33,
155

Whether you go to college or university straight from school, study part-time, or return to study full-time after a period in other employment, to get the most out of your course you will need to develop effective learning skills. Whatever subjects you are studying, the practical advice in this guide will help you to achieve your goals.

Part One: Accepting responsibility for your learning will help you to look after yourself, organise your time and avoid stress.
Part Two: Student centred learning will help you to develop your ability to think, and to learn by listening, discussing, observing and writing.
Part Three: Revision and examination techniques will help you to learn and revise your work and to approach tests and examinations with confidence.

The clear straightforward advice will help you to keep fit for study, use effective learning techniques, and communicate your thoughts in assessed course work, tests and examinations. As well as these features, which contributed to the success of the first edition, this second edition includes more advice on working in groups, finding information, citing sources, and on using a computer to help you prepare essays, project reports, and short talks or presentations.

Robert Barrass has many years experience of helping students on degree and diploma courses at the University of Sunderland to improve their writing and other key skills. His best selling books on key skills include *Students Must Write* and *Scientists Must Write*, as well as *Study!*, all of which are published by Routledge – as is his new book, *Writing at Work*.